UNTO CAESAR

Unto Caesar

The Political Relevance of Christianity

DAVID McLELLAN

University of Notre Dame Press

Notre Dame   London

Copyright © 1993 by
University of Notre Dame Press
Notre Dame, Indiana 46556
All Rights Reserved

Library of Congress Cataloging-in-Publication Data

McLellan, David.
    Unto Caesar : the political relevance of Christianity / David
McLellan.
        p.   cm. — (Loyola lectures in political analysis)
    Includes bibliographical references and index.
    ISBN 0-268-01900-2
    1. Christianity and politics —History of doctrines—20th century.
I. Title.   II. Series.
BR115.P7M33145   1992
261.7'0904–dc20   92-53753
                                                                  CIP

Manufactured in the United States of America

Contents

Preface

This book originated as the Covey Lectures in Political Analysis given at Loyola University in Chicago. I am grateful to Frank Covey for his financial support and to Richard Hartigan and his colleagues in the Department of Political Science for providing such a congenial and stimulating environment. Much of the research incorporated into this book, particularly in Chapter 2, was helped by a grant from the Nuffield Foundation and I wish to record my thanks to Patricia Thomas there for her helpful cooperation. And Jean Gil's sense of logistics and organization has been, as usual, invaluable.

David McLellan
Canterbury, 1991

1
Unto Caesar:
The Political Relevance
of Christianity

> Religious faith seems to be not only the mirror of a soci-
> ety; it can also create conditions for not coinciding with it.
> In this way religious faith can be a window as well as a mir-
> ror: it keeps open the sense that society should be differ-
> ent. Thus, in times of crisis, religion can become a
> breeding ground for the self criticism of a society.
> H. M. Kuitert

Over the last decade the political importance of religion
has become more evident than many would have predicted
in the 1950s and 1960s. In North America the arrival of
Jimmy Carter in the presidency provided evangelical Christians with a sense of legitimate political mission. Christian
duty and responsible citizenship were once again united and
the 1980s saw the rise of the New Christian Right which,
although it seems to have peaked around 1986, achieved a
dismayingly high level of political influence. In South America we see the spread of liberation theology, a radical Catholicism drawing on Marxist social analysis, and in Eastern
Europe the role of the churches in fostering the movements
of opposition is widely known. Even in the comparatively
secular enclave of the United Kingdom, it is not only the
reaction of some Muslims to *The Satanic Verses* that has

1

brought the question of the relationship of religion to public authority to the fore: there has recently been a surprisingly sharp attack on the values underlying the British government's education policies by the leader of England's Roman Catholics, Cardinal Hume, and a fresh assault on the same government's neglect of inner cities that has placed fresh strains on relations between Downing Street and the Anglican establishment. The original report *Faith in the City* published in 1985 was described by Cabinet Ministers as "pure Marxist theology"—an evidence of their depth of disagreement if also of their ignorance both of theology and of Marxism.

Against this background, the aim of this introductory chapter is to offer a general discussion of the relevance to politics of religion—and particularly the Christian religion as this is the only one likely to be familiar to most of my readers, and certainly myself. In so doing I do not intend to provide answers to these very vexing questions, though it will no doubt be clear where my own preferences lie. My aim is the more modest one of trying to sketch out a framework that will perhaps enable us all to reflect more fruitfully on these matters. To this end, I want briefly to review the classical political theoretical tradition where it deals with the questions; then, to discuss the view that Christianity is irrelevant to politics either because it just is so, being other-worldly, or because, in as far as it is this-worldly, it is simply a reflection of political arrangements and therefore has no relevance in the sense of being an independent variable. Third, I will suggest, more substantially, that religion is not solely a dependent variable but has some substantial influence at times on the society in which we live and therefore is a fitting subject of interest for all, whether they be believers or not. Fourth, I shall have a few negative words to say about the view that, although religion may well in fact *be* influential, this is inappropriate in a liberal democracy. Finally, after some rather caustic remarks on Margaret Thatcher's version of Christianity, I shall conclude by sketching out what does seem to me to be a suitable dialectic between politics and religion. These remarks are intended to set the scene for the "case studies" which follow and which are designed to illustrate these general themes in specific instances.

The founding father of all thought on this subject in the Christian West is undoubtedly Augustine. However indifferent and even hostile to the state early Christians such as Tertullian may have been, the adoption under Constantine of Christianity as the official religion of the Empire posed the question of the appropriate relationship of church and state that has been with us ever since. Augustine's answer, in the famous nineteenth chapter of *The City of God* is in terms of two cities, the heavenly and the earthly, which are in fact two societies, that of the saved and that of the reprobate. This makes Augustine's answer capable of many interpretations, for the two cities are by no means co-extensive respectively with church and state.[1]

Mainstream Christianity has seen the state as, in some sense, divinely ordained. In Augustine the state is a result of the Fall and a bulwark against sin; in Aquinas, more optimistically, it is part of the natural created order; even in Luther with his very strong separation of the two kingdoms, spiritual and secular, the authority of the state derived ultimately from God. The classical political theorists do not depart from this tradition. Machiavelli, in his *Discourses*, saw religion as a strong political cement and declared that "the princes of a republic or a kingdom must maintain the foundations of the religion they have; and having done this, it will be an easy thing for them to keep their republic religious, and in consequence, good and unified."[2] We may or may not accept the argument of Howard Warrender who reduces all obligation in Hobbes to an ultimate obligation to obey God,[3] but there is undoubtedly a strong analogy in Hobbes's thought between the role of the sovereign and that of God. Hobbes can refer to Leviathan itself as a "mortal God."[4] According to Locke, "all legitimate authority everywhere and always exercised by one human being over another is an

authority conferred upon that person ultimately by God."[5]
Locke's whole theory of rights depends on his view of the
universe as divinely created.[6] Although Rousseau might, at
first sight, seem to put forward a very radical form of Christianity, in practice he is ultra-conservative and his proposals
for a civil religion are designed simply to uphold the sanctity
of the social contract and the laws. Indeed, it almost seems to
be a professional tendency of political theorists to subordinate religion to politics.

Another view, that religion is and should be separate from
politics only came into prominence in post-Enlightenment
societies.[7] This view has constantly been supported by reference to the text "Render therefore unto Caesar the things
that are Caesar's and unto God the things that are God's." The
rules of God, in other words, are one thing, those of politics
and the state are another: separate spheres. But it should be
noted that the Christian tradition has, from Tertullian
onwards, offered a slightly different interpretation. On the
several occasions in which the wily Pharisees try to entrap
him, Jesus usually responds by undermining the presuppositions of the question. The word render—*apodote* in the
Greek original—is better translated "give back," return to
the source from which it came. Just as the penny should be
given back to Caesar since it bears his image, so to God
should be given back what bears God's image—that is,
humankind made in God's image and likeness. The *and* in
"*and* unto God the things that are God's" has the sense of
but: give pennies to Caesar, *but* yourself to God, an overriding obligation which might be thought to include and indeed
subordinate the political.[8]

But this merely reveals the text to be ambiguous. Complex
questions are, of course, rarely resolved by appeals to texts,
slogans, or even principles, so I now wish to examine in a
broader context the two positions outlined above. Take first
the view that Christianity is (and possibly should be) irrelevant to politics, on the grounds that the same version of Christianity is compatible with very different political positions.

Examples from the history of the United States might be adduced in support of this position. The early Pentecostalists of the nineteenth century were left-leaning with a rhetoric not far from that of the International Workers of the World, but after 1920 they became political conservatives—anti-evolution, anti-communist, and anti-Al Smith—without any change in their religious doctrines.[9] In the antebellum South fundamentalist Protestants did not want their biblically inspired moral views to be embodied in legislation, but they have held very different views on that question in the 1980s.[10] Or consider Mary Fulbrook's discussion in *Pietism and Politics* of the very different contributions made by the Puritan and Pietist movements to the success or failure of absolutist rule in England, in Wurttemberg, and in Prussia where the same religious ideas and aspirations led to quite different political attitudes and alliances depending, so she claims, on the structural context.[11] In more recent times, both Jesse Jackson and Jerry Falwell lay claim to the support of the evangelical Protestant tradition.

But even in these examples, note that Christianity is not, strictly speaking, irrelevant to politics. The most that is being claimed is that, in these instances, it is not the specific content of the religious beliefs that is efficacious in determining a particular political outcome. Religion, that is, plays a role (sometimes a crucial role) in the political process, but the fact that it can play this role is not due to the particular religious doctrines but to the general context in which they were deployed: religious belief was still a necessary condition for the relevant political outcome even though the religious belief was itself moulded by the political context. Scientists may (mistakenly) claim to be apolitical but theologians cannot even try to do so. Theology is inevitably involved with social science. The demand that bishops adopt the same attitude to economists that the pope should have adopted to Galileo—respect for the professional expert—is based on a fallacious assimilation of social to natural science. Even the expertise of natural science is too often invoked to occlude discussion of different political options: the questionability of social science "experts" should follow *a fortiori*. Indeed, the view that Christianity, as an other-worldly religion concerned with personal redemption, is devoid of political content seems to be just wishful thinking. It is a view propounded by that preeminently wishful thinker J.-J. Rousseau who, in his *Social Contract*, declared: "Christianity as a religion is entirely spiritual, occupied solely with heavenly things; the country of the Christian is not of the world. It is true that he does his duty; but he does so with profound indifference to the good or ill success of his efforts."[12] Various forms of contemporary existentialist theology have continued this attitude and concerned themselves almost exclusively with the authenticity of existence in interpersonal relationships. Rousseau's view has recently been reiterated by Edward Norman in his controversial Reith Lectures of 1979. But even this approach itself has inescapable political implications, and of a conservative nature. It is no accident, as the Marxists like to say, that Norman was Dean of the highly conservative Cambridge college of Peterhouse. And we should not forget that politics is relevant to Christianity. The very survival of the Christian religion depends on its collective memory as embodied in its language, ritual, artifacts, etc. The preservation of these depends, at least in part, on political arrangements and the retention of the social power to ensure their preservation.[13]

If, then, Christianity is condemned to have some political relevance, what is the nature of that relevance? (I leave aside here the extreme views of such thinkers as Voegelin, Dawson, or even Berdiayev who see all political systems of which they disapprove as, at bottom, a species of religious heresy:[14] they represent a version of my thesis, but in far too strong a form.) One, but not the only, positive version of the connection between Christianity and politics is as a reflection and legitimation of the structure of political power. And this is often allied to a thesis about the social determination of religious beliefs of which traditional, orthodox Marxism is the starkest expression. Marxism tends to restrict religion's relevance to a minimum by dismissing religion as an instrument of class rule, an ideological bulwark of the dominant class. This view contains a covert ontology, both in the simplistic equation of the origin of a belief with its truth value and in its assumption that religious assertions must always be a cloak for something else—obviously so in the case of conservative religion but equally so in the case of radical religious movements such as Anabaptists or Polynesian Cargo Cults which must cloak political demands. The traditional Marxist metaphor from heavy engineering—base and superstructure—tends to put religion on the tip-top of the superstructure and thus at the farthest remove from "reality."

Functional accounts of religion following Durkheim, though capable of greater subtlety, go even further in denying autonomy to the religious sphere and indeed deny any substantive content to the notion of religion. The definition of religion here as society's ideal self-description is too wide for my purposes. Yet even if we give the notion of religion a more substantive content, we can see that there is much truth in Durkheim's approach. In the rather less static version of it proposed by Robert Bellah, there are striking parallels between the religious dynamism and the economic dynamism of the United States.[15] Images of God *do* often mirror existing dispositions of political authority. For Nietzsche, the levelling mediocrity of modern democracy was just a secularization of the slave mentality of Christianity that he so despised. Much liberal Protestant theology in the United States has been devoted to dismantling ideas of an autarchic and monarchical God in favor of a more federal-democratic conception.[16] In this regard the pragmatic ideas of James and Dewey were taken up by Whitehead to reveal a picture of God not as the un-moved mover—the great Before who created the universe *ex nihilo*—but as someone who continually brings order out of chaos (*e pluribus unum!*) in some sort of dynamic interdependence with the universe. Whitehead rightly said that in post-Constantinian Christendom "the

Church gave unto God the attributes which belonged exclusively to Caesar";[17] what he did not realize was that the many
process philosophers and theologians of his own day were
doing exactly the same.

Or, to move across the Atlantic, consider the images of
God which have accompanied the rise of the welfare state in
Britain over the last century and more. Here both liberal
progressive theology and political theory coincide in depict-
ing both God and the state in terms of bureaucratic benevo-
lence. As the contemporary state has increasingly taken over
and coordinated the functions of patronage and of charity
that previously rested in disparate private hands, so the
monolithic God of Protestantism has come to usurp all the
various tasks, protective and entrepreneurial, that had previously lain in the hands of angels and saints. As one writer has
recently put it, "today God is thought of by many as the
celestial grandmother indulgently handing out benefits and
performing more satisfactorily the role which an under-
financed welfare state tried vainly to fulfill."[18]

Yet the opposite is also true: however often religion may
be no more than the flowers on the chain, the halo above the
valley of tears, it can also be the sigh of the oppressed creature, the heart of a heartless world—and in a more effective
sense than Marx intended. Conceptions of God can serve as
a conscious focus of opposition to prevailing ideas and
arrangements—images of an alternative society. We need
only think of the emergence of black theologies, particularly
in the United States, which refuse to accept the white man's
God. Or, more radically, feminist theologies which find ludi-
crous the idea of a God who, as in the traditional story of the
fall of Lucifer, could mind that an angel should try to fly
higher than Him—the word "Him" being, of course, used
here advisedly. To take a narrower and more specific example:
it has been plausibly argued that immediately prior to the
1935 general election in New Zealand "the religious variable
exerted considerable independent influence on social
change, by legitimating the agents of change—the Labour

Party—and by suggesting specific innovations that the Labour Party might adopt in order to bring about a specifically Christian solution to the problem.... It was by producing religious symbols to interpret the situation that the religious institutions exerted an independent influence on the changes that occurred."[19] Here the role of religion, and particularly theology, is that of producing symbols which legitimize otherwise unpopular beliefs, and thus enable them to gain increasing acceptance. Although religious belief rarely determines outcomes, the affinity between religion and socio-political attitudes pointed out by such writers as de Toqueville and Weber does afford religion an influence that is often underestimated.

That this influence should be possible involves conceding that religious belief can act as a partially independent variable in the social and political process. Both the Marxist and the Durkheimian traditions find it difficult to concede this. The anarchist tradition, however, has taken religion much more seriously: recall the lengthy polemics of Proudhon and Bakunin against the idea of God as necessarily authoritarian or of Nietzsche against the idea of God as necessarily weak. The point here is that theology can be both a dependent *and* independent variable: theology and religious belief in general are socially constructed realities, but that means that they are both socially constructed *and* social realities. The most important doctrinal controversy in the early history of the Christian church was the Arian heresy which revolved around the question of whether Jesus was of like substance to the Father or of one substance—Homoousios or Homoiousios, the difference of a single letter. That an argument about a single letter could be so prolonged, so bitter, and so threatening to the very foundations of the Roman Empire may seem to some like a species of collective dementia.[20] Not so. The Arians by denying Godhead to Jesus left God the Father as an isolated Emperor in heaven best represented by a solitary tyrant on earth. A strong form of Trinitarian doctrine, by contrast, offers space for a more pluralist kind of politics. To take an example from nearer home: different interpretations of Protestantism produce different conclusions about the value of involvement in politics. Whereas the Baptist 'free will' tradition still makes the average church member in the United States reluctant to see religious doctrines carried through into politics, the Calvinist tradition, which is far stronger in the North of Ireland than in the United States, leads to a tendency for the saints to impose their version of righteousness on the unregenerate.[21]

Although religious belief does in fact affect people's political attitudes, it might be argued this influence is inappropriate in a liberal democracy and we should strive for its elimination. In a liberal democratic society, in other words, the grounds of decision should have an interpersonal validity that extends to virtually all members of society. Decisions should be based on shared premises or types of reasoning that are accessible to everyone. Although the theories of liberal democracy advanced by John Rawls and Bruce Ackerman do not explicitly mention religion, its exclusion is implied. In Rawls, for example, the "veil of ignorance" behind which people are to choose the principles of justice which will govern their society includes ignorance of their particular conceptions of the good. More recently Rawls has written: "In public questions ways of reasoning and rules of evidence for reaching true general beliefs that help settle whether institutions are just should be of a kind everyone can recognize,"[22] which seems to exclude religion. But it seems to me simply untrue that important political questions can be resolved on the basis of value premises that are shared by all or even on shared approaches to factual knowledge. To see the force of this, one has only to reflect on the arguments surrounding such issues as the possession of nuclear weapons, our attitude to the environment, or to abortion. Unfortunately, in very many important issues rational grounds for assessing what is true are highly inconclusive. In such cases people are likely to rely on some sort of deep and intuitive feelings, and this often involves a religious perspective. To say this is not to undermine any vital premise of liberal democracy: it is to recognize the fact that citizens in a liberal democracy rely generally on moral judgments to arrive at decisions, and that moral judgments are frequently informed by religious views. It is also to recognize that liberal democracy is less anemic than many of its proponents would have us believe. Yet this recognition is also compatible with the view that, as far as open public discussion is concerned, it is mistaken for the ordinary citizen to advocate a position by direct reference to his or her religious values—general human welfare being the appropriate point of reference. Where individuals get their values is up to them: the terms in which individuals advocate their values to fellow-citizens is more circumscribed.[23] If one were a church leader whose job is to express the views of a specifically *religious* community, the case would be, of course, different. But, by contrast, the tendency of *political* leaders to refer to the deity should be resisted—because of both the tendency to homogenize religion and the usually arrogant presupposition of the coincidence of their country's progress with the purposes of God.

An arresting example of what can happen if the above warning is not heeded is provided by Margaret Thatcher. She is quoted as saying that, if the churches took sides on practical issues, "this can only weaken the influence and independence of the church, whose members ideally should help the thinking of all political parties"; which seems to amount to saying that the churches can be very influential so long as they do not actually try to influence anything. This reminds me of the non-apocryphal churchwardens writing a letter to the bishop about the type of person they hoped would be appointed to the vacant post of parish priest: "Our experience and reports we have heard of politically active clergy in this part of the county compel us to believe that such a ministry would be neither beneficial nor fruitful."[24] Underlying this utterance is the assumption that being a supporter of the Conservative Party is not to be politically active.

According to Margaret Thatcher, in her speech to the General Assembly of the Scottish Church in 1988, the distinctive marks of Christianity stem not from the social but

from the spiritual side of our lives (note the sharp
dichotomy). They consist in a triad of belief: in the doctrine
of Free Will, in the divinely created sovereignty of individual
conscience, and in the crucifixion as the supreme and exemplary act of choice. They all, you will note, boil down to the
individual's right to choose—Christ's choosing to die on the
Cross is merely the forerunner of those who have chosen to
buy their own council house, occupy pay-beds in National
Health Service hospitals, or send their children to private
schools.[25] And in outlining her views about the relevance of
Christianity to public policy—the things, as she puts it, that
are Caesar's—she gives a breezy summary of both the Old
and the New Testaments and finds therein another three key
elements: a view of the universe, a proper attitude to work,
and principles to shape social and economic life.

While a "view of the universe" merely sounds as though it
were an attractive and desirable amenity, like a view of the
sea, "the proper attitude to work" gets more down to it.
Here, together with the principles that shape social and economic life Mrs. Thatcher might, vainly, have hoped to establish common ground with her audience who were, after all,
grounded in the Calvinist tradition. For, to quote Raban,
"like Calvin himself, Mrs. Thatcher will have no truck with
mediating institutions. On this, the record of her government
is both logical and exemplary, with its attacks on the Church,
the BBC, and the universities, on powerful agencies of local
government like the Greater London Council, and even
(especially over South African sanctions) on the monarchy.
She is passionately 'anti-statist'—yet every institution which
has traditionally stood between the individual and central
government has been either abolished or has come under
heavy fire from her administration. If the Kingdom of Man is
a shadowy reflection of the Kingdom of God, then Margaret
Thatcher is a good Calvinist; for it is emerging as a fundamental principle of 'Thatcherism' that individuals shall stand
as nakedly before their Government as they do before their
Maker."[26]

There is too close a relationship here between religion and politics. Mrs. Thatcher's narrow, thin, simple, petit-bourgeois (in the worse sense) attitude to economics and politics has colonized the religious sphere and impoverished it almost beyond belief. Its American equivalent is the evangelical Christian who is quoted as saying: "'Give and you'll be given unto' is the fundamental practical principle of the Christian life, and when there's no private property you can't give it because you don't own it.... Socialism is inherently hostile to Christianity and Capitalism is simply the essential mode of human life that corresponds to religious truth."[27] *All* this kind of politicization of religion—like that of art and literature—is to be resisted. But, and this is my argument, it cannot be resisted by relegating religion to a separate sphere. It is just not possible: the two are substantially connected. A jejune politics (and Thatcher has a *very* jejune approach to politics) will yield a jejune religion. But the reverse is also true: a bigoted or superficial or not sufficiently materialist religion will equally have a deleterious effect on politics. From this point of view the dictum of Marx needs to be reversed and the criticism of politics needs to issue in the criticism of theology; and those inside churches must make sure that their own organizations and practices at least come up to the level of the standards that they are advocating for society at large.

If Tertullian's interpretation of my text is right and men and women are made in God's image, they should enjoy the maximum of effective freedom. But, in Britain and elsewhere, this freedom is currently being taken away from local government, from the universities, from Trade Unions, as power becomes ever more centralized in Westminster, Whitehall, and the City of London. And the churches are being asked to legitimize this process by preaching traditional moral values to shore up an ever stronger state. Under these circumstances it would be a mistake for those who oppose such policies and values to fail to leave some space for religion in their approach to society and politics. In the long run, religions are difficult to coopt and their essential values are not readily corrupted by power. It is, I believe, significant that at the end of 1989 the demonstrations in Dresden and Leipzig rested on a base in the Lutheran church and that the guerrillas of El Salvador depend crucially on their church's base communities. Although, nearer home, the intellectuals and cosmopolitan elites may be steeped in post-modernism, religion—charismatic and evangelical—stalks the inner cities. It may be, as MacIntyre has forcefully argued, that so many of our modern aporias spring from the fact that our moral sense has been uprooted from any shared tradition of belief and story about our past.[28] But religion in some shape or form has been a deep and enduring aspect of human activity, and there is every reason to think that this will continue for at least the near future. Benign neglect or outright rejection by the left will mean that the immense power of religion can be captured by the ideologies of the right. Consider here the recent role of the so-called "moral majority" in America and the way in which, almost by default, a whole string of repressive social measures from welfare cuts to the regulation of sexual mores appear to many there to have behind them the weight of the whole Judeo-Christian tradition.

My argument is that, however the Judeo-Christian tradition is understood (and I think it is oppositional rather than establishment), it is possible, legitimate, and advisable to use that tradition to afford a critical perspective on the political problems of the present time. The most apparently abstract metaphysical beliefs are, at the same time, severely practical. Thus the notorious polemic of William James towards the end of his *Varieties of Religious Experience* is misplaced. James pours scorn on "the metaphysical attributes of God" and claims that "from the point of view of practical religion, the metaphysical monster which they offer to our worship is an absolutely worthless invention of the scholarly mind."[29] James's view is, of course, a function of his own, equally metaphysical, brand of Cartesian individualism. All politics involves metaphysical choice.[30] This could be illustrated by large-scale survey research,[31] but my concern here is rather with individual thinkers. The following case studies are intended to illustrate this inescapable correlation between theology—images of God—and anthropology—images of human society.

Notes

1. See further P. Brown, "Political Society," in *Augustine: A Collection of Critical Essays,* ed. R. Markus (Garden City: Doubleday, 1972).

2. *The Discourses of Nicolo Machiavelli,* ed. L. Walker (London: RKP, 1975) vol. 1, p. 244. See also S. De Grazia, *Machiavelli in Hell* (Princeton: Princeton University Press, 1989), 119, 376.

3. Cf. H. Warrender, *The Political Philosophy of Hobbes: His Theory of Obligation* (Oxford: Clarendon Press). See also W. Glover, "God and Thomas Hobbes," in *Hobbes Studies,* ed. K. Brown (Oxford: Blackwell, 1965).

4. T. Hobbes, *Leviathan* (Oxford: Blackwell, 1957), 107.

5. J. Locke, *Two Treatises of Civil Government* (Cambridge: Cambridge University Press, 1970), 143.

6. See further J. Dunn, *Interpreting Political Responsibility* (Princeton: Princeton University Press, 1990), chap. 2.

7. See J. Crimmins, ed., *Religion, Secularization, and Political Thought: From Thomas Hobbes to J. S. Mill* (London: Routledge, 1989).

8. For a summary of recent exegetical research, see F. Bruce "Render Unto Caesar," in *Jesus and the Politics of His Day,* ed. E. Bammel and C. Moule (Cambridge: Cambridge University Press, 1984).

9. R. Laurence Moore, *Religious Outsiders and the Making of Americans* (New York: Oxford University Press, 1986), 144.

10. Ibid., 156.

11. Cf. M. Fulbrook, *Piety and Politics: Religion and the Rise of Absolutism in England, Wurttemberg, and Prussia* (Cambridge: Cambridge University Press, 1983), 174.

12. J.-J. Rousseau, *The Social Contract and Discourses* (New York: Dutton, 1973), 274.

13. Cf. N. Lash, *Theology on the Way to Emmaeus* (London: Trinity Press, 1986), 70.

14. See J. Shklar, *After Utopia: The Decline of Political Faith* (Princeton: Princeton University Press, 1969), 170.

15. See further R. Bellah, *The Broken Covenant: American Civil Religion in a Time of Trial* (New York: Seabury Press, 1975).

16. Cf. D. Nicholls, *Diety and Domination: Images of God and the State in the Nineteenth and Twentieth Centuries* (London: Routledge, 1989), chap. 5.

17. A. N. Whitehead, *Process and Reality* (New York: Free Press, 1978), 342.

18. Nicholls, *Diety and Domination,* 30.

19. J. Brown, *New Zealand Journal of Political Science* 54 (1976): 33.

20. See, for example, the ironical commentary of Gibbon in *Decline and Fall of the Roman Empire,* ed. Burg (London: Methuen, 1896), vol. 2, p. 344.

21. For a stout defense of the claim that the conflict in Northern Ireland is, among other things, a deeply *religious* conflict, see P. Badham, *The Contribution of Religion to the Conflict in Northern Ireland* (Canterbury: Centre for the Study of Religion and Society, 1988).

22. J. Rawls, "Kantian Constructivism in Moral Theory: The Dewey Lectures," *Journal of Philosophy* 77 (1980): 539.

23. For an excellent discussion, see K. Greenwalt, *Public Policy and Individual Choice* (New York: Oxford University Press, 1989).

24. Quoted in P. Hinchliffe, *Holiness and Politics* (London: Darton, Longman and Todd, 1982), 6.

25. I am merely summarizing here the splendidly amusing and incisive critique of the Thatcher speech by Jonathan Raban in his *God, Man, and Mrs. Thatcher* (London: Chatto and Windus, 1989).

26. Ibid., 34.

27. George Gilder, speech-writer to Ronald Reagan, quoted in R. Wuthnow, *The Restructuring of American Religion: Society and Faith since World War II* (Princeton: Princeton University Press, 1988), 248.

28. See A. MacIntyre, *Whose Justice: Which Rationality?* (Notre Dame, Ind.: University of Notre Dame Press, 1988).

29. W. James, *Varieties of Religious Experience* (New York: Random, 1990).

30. Cf. J. Maritain, *Le Philosophe dans le cite* (Mulhouse: Alsatia 1960), 9.

31. See, for example, the discussion in K. Wald, *Religion and Politics in the United States* (New York: St. Martin's Press, 1987), 77.

Further Reading

Cullman, Oscar. *The State in the New Testament*. London: SCM Press, 1957.

Fulbrook, Mary. *Piety and Politics: Religion and the Rise of Absolutism in England, Wurttemberg and Prussia*. Cambridge: Cambridge University Press, 1983.

Gill, Robin. *The Social Context of Theology*. Oxford: Mowbrays, 1975.

———. *Theology and Social Structure*. Oxford: Mowbrays, 1977.

Habgood, John. *Church and Nation in a Secular Age*. London: Darton, Longman and Todd, 1983.

Hauerwas, Stanley. *The Peaceable Kingdom: A Primer in Christian Ethics*. Notre Dame, Ind.: University of Notre Dame Press, 1985.

Hinchliff, Peter. *Holiness and Politics*. London: Darton, Longman and Todd, 1982.

Hunsinger, George. Ed. and trans. *Karl Barth and Radical Politics*. Louisville, Ky.: Westminster Press, 1976.

Kantorowicz, Ernst. *The King's Two Bodies: A Study in Mediaeval Political Theology*. Princeton: Princeton University Press, 1957.

Medhurst, Kenneth, and George Moyser. *Church and Politics in a Secular Age*. Oxford: Clarendon Press, 1988.

Moore, R. Laurence. *Religious Outsiders and the Making of Americans*. New York: Oxford University Press, 1986.

Nicholls, David. *Deity and Domination: Images of God and the State in the Nineteenth and Twentieth Centuries*. London: Routledge, 1989.

Raban, Jonathan. *God, Man and Mrs. Thatcher.* London: Chatto and Windus, 1989.

Shklar, Judith. *After Utopia: The Decline of Political Faith.* Princeton: Princeton University Press, 1969.

Suggate, Alan. *William Temple and Christian Social Ethics Today.* Edinburgh: T. and T. Clark, 1987.

Viner, Jacob. *The Role of Providence in the Social Order: An Essay in Intellectual History.* Princeton: Princeton University Press, 1972.

Williams, Rowan. *Arius: Heresy and Tradition.* London: Darton, Longman and Todd, 1987.

2

Conservative Politics: Simone Weil

It is only by entering the transcendental, the supernatural, the authentically spiritual order that man rises above the social. Until then, whatever he may do, the social is transcendent in relation to him.

Simone Weil

The inevitable interconnection between religion and politics is at its clearest in the thought of the religious mystic and political philosopher Simone Weil. Most of those who develop mystical tendencies reject the secular world: Weil continued to hold fast, in a sometimes desperate tension, both to her mystical beliefs and to her political commitments. She has been rightly described as "a unique example in this century of Christian Platonist mystical speculation."[1] Weil's Christian Platonism is a necessary—indeed, almost a sufficient—condition for the emergence of much of her later political thought, all of which is entirely subordinate to her conception of God. Although Weil is an extremely idiosyncratic thinker, it would not be misleading to characterize her later political thought as conservative. She was certainly implacably opposed to the ideas of change and progress so firmly entrenched in the world views of bourgeois democracy and its offspring, classical Marxism. This opposition was firmly rooted in the Platonic belief in the existence of absolute, eternal values opposed to, or at least entirely separate from, the

21

way of the world. Throughout history, Platonism has had two sides to it: a radical one that appeals to eternal and absolute values as against those of the status quo and a conservative one in that Platonism's eventual goal is a static society governed by an elite of the wise and the good. The proposal for rule by philosophers in Plato's *Republic* exhibits both these facets, and Weil's ideas are an attempt to adapt the principles of the *Republic* to twentieth-century France.

Weil did not start out as a conservative: it was conversion to her own peculiar form of Catholic Christianity (together, of course, with her experience of French politics in the 1930s) that led her to a revision of her earlier anarcho-syndicalism. Born in 1909 into a middle-class Jewish family, she was an outstanding philosophy student in the Paris of the 1920s. Jean-Paul Sartre, Simone de Beauvoir, Claude Levi-Strauss were her contemporaries and her equals. She spent several years as a philosophy teacher in various French lycees. This was the time of the Great Depression and her passionate commitment to ideals of social justice led her to become active in the Trade Union movement. Finding that left-wing politics did not live up to its own ideals, she decided to become a worker herself and spent a year as an unskilled machinist in, among others, Renault in Paris. She joined the anarchist side in the Spanish Civil War, but was soon invalided out. After a brief return to school-teaching, the outbreak of war forced her to flee with her parents to Marseilles where they spent almost two years before getting passage to New York. Simone Weil then managed to recross the Atlantic and join the Free French in London. Her health soon failed owing to her extremely ascetic life-style and tuberculosis. She died in a sanatorium in Ashford, Kent in the summer of 1943. During this short life, she wrote incessantly. Her collected works, which are now in the course of publication, will amount to eighteen large volumes ranging widely over politics and spirituality. She saw the advance of technology as bringing about a specialized technocratic society that threatened individual liberty both in the East and in the West. After a series of mystical experiences in the mid-1930s, she complemented her political writings by meditations on the meaning of the Passion of Christ, the relationship of Christianity to Eastern religions, and the nature of God. In the last few months of her life, while employed by the Free French in London, Weil wrote extensively for de Gaulle on the shape of post-war politics in France.

Some have claimed to see a sharp break between a pre-conversion "political" Weil and a post-conversion "spiritual" Weil, but she continued until the end of her life to be passionately interested in politics. The last six months of her life, in particular, produced some of her most incisive writing on politics. These writings share themes with her earlier work, but deal more explicitly with the connection between politics and religion. Thus it is these writings that chiefly concern us here—particularly the book-length piece entitled *The Need for Roots*. This was Weil's most extensive political work. It was commissioned by the Free French in London and designed to provide a philosophical and historical background to the reconstruction of French society that would be possible following the victory of the Allies. Weil centered her proposals for reconstruction around the human need for roots which she saw as the most pressing need of post-war French (and indeed any) society—uprootedness being the characteristic bane of modern societies. What did it mean to be rooted? She wrote: "A human being has roots by virtue of his real, active and natural participation in the life of a community which preserves in living shape certain particular treasures of the past and certain particular expectations for the future."[2] Such roots were being increasingly corroded by the power of money and the influence of the profit motive as well as by an education system whose principles were technical, compartmentalized, and pragmatic. The resulting lack of roots was all the more dangerous as it was self-propagating: the uprooted tended to uproot others. Rome and Israel were examples of this in the ancient world and, in more recent times, Hitler's Germany and the whole European colonial enterprise.

The result of a lack of roots was a society in which only two bonds of attachment among individuals remained: the nation-state and the cash nexus. The bond of the nation-state had replaced the increasingly nuclear family, professional associations, or local communities as the focus of its members' loyalty. Always supremely anti-nationalist and anti-statist, Weil reserved her worst scorn for the state which was "a cold concern which cannot inspire love, but itself kills, suppresses everything that might be loved; so one is forced to love it, because there is nothing else."[3] The result of this ambivalent attitude to the state was that while there was a tendency to talk idolatrously of "eternal France," at the same time "no Frenchman has the slightest qualms about robbing or cheating the state in the matter of customs, taxes, subsidies or anything else."[4] The development of the state had exhausted the country on which it battened and France had become the curious phenomenon of a democracy in which all public institutions were hated and despised by the entire population. Thus contemporary society, together with its typical product the nation-state, viewed history as inevitable progress and tended to glorify force—history being written of course, by the powerful whose successful use of force was inevitably self-described as progressive. In such a society the idea of justice, which Weil defined as "behaving exactly as though there were equality when one is stronger in an unequal relationship," was bound to be degraded since "where force is absolutely sovereign, justice is absolutely unreal."[5] Its typically jejune intellectual products were classical economic liberalism, which vainly imagined that justice might be the result of the force of money and the market, and Marxism, which relegated justice to a sphere beyond the class struggle. Underpinning all this was the unchallengeable position accorded to modern science. Since the Renaissance the very conception of science had been that of a branch of study whose object was placed beyond good and evil. Weil was not against the scientific endeavor as such. What she opposed was the false prestige given to science under the illusion that it could, of itself, ever deliver any sort of genuine meaning or truth to life. Truth was an aspect of absolute goodness and only to be approached through a kind of loving attention that was quite different from a desire to acquire knowledge.

Thus far the grim diagnosis. The remedies that Weil proposed for what she regarded as the probably terminal illnesses of modern civilization were threefold: a reevaluation of the role of work in society, a reformulation of the bases of political power, and a restoration of the supremacy of spiritual values.

The discovery of the dignity of manual labor was, in Weil's opinion, the one and only spiritual advance made on the civilization of the ancient Greeks. The peculiar mission of our age was the creation of a civilization founded upon the spiritual nature of work. There were hints of it in Rousseau, Sand, Tolstoy, Proudhon, Marx, and the papal encyclicals. A long-term project for achieving this new civilization would probably include the abolition of large factories and joint-stock companies and a transfer of the ownership of machines to cooperatives. The advent of the electronic age and of automated machinery presented opportunities for decentralized cooperative production and workers' control of the production process. In the countryside, the depopulation of the land and the colonial attitude of the city to country could only be cured by the transfer of land ownership exclusively to those who worked it, whether privately or cooperatively. Weil, like her heroes Plato and Rousseau, began with the importance of education whose inspiration was to be sought "like the method itself, among the truths eternally inscribed in the nature of things."[6] With a reform of education and indeed of the whole contemporary idea of culture, school and further education should be closely integrated with the work process, with working hours reduced accordingly.[7]

In her proposals for the foundation of France's Fourth
Republic, contained in articles written at the same time as
The Need for Roots, Weil canvased many ideas, some of them
distinctly bizarre. One of her principal aims was to minimize
the powers of the legislative assembly and to prevent the
return of the political parties "whose total capture of public
life is what has done us so much damage."[8] What was important for her was not so much electoral arrangements as how
those who held power were to be limited, judged, and if necessary, punished. Following the political philosophy of her
erstwhile teacher Alain she held that it was ridiculous to sup-
pose that the whole people could govern, but they *could* set
limits to the powers of those who did. Her sketch of a possible constitution (which she admitted would take over two
generations to evolve) contained the following suggestions:
that a president for life be chosen by senior magistrates from
among their number; that the president choose a prime minister for five years; that the prime minister could be
arraigned before the supreme court in case of misdemeanor
and in any case would have to answer before a judicial tribunal at the end of office; that a legislative assembly be
elected every five years, and that, similarly, any members not
re-elected should pass before a tribunal to have their conduct reviewed; that the judiciary should mediate serious con-
flicts between legislature and executive; that every twenty
years there should be a national referendum on the character
of public life, preceded by a period of serious reflection
devoid of any sort of propaganda or campaigning; and that, if
the result of the referendum was to declare public life unsat-
isfactory, the president should be deprived of office and a
suitable punishment, including the possibility of death,
inflicted.

Inside such a framework it might be possible, she felt, to
achieve a genuine equality which "consists in a recognition,
at once public, general, effective and genuinely expressed in
institutions and custom, that the same amount of respect and
consideration is due to every human being because this

respect is due to the human being as such and is not a matter of degree."[9] Unbridled equality of opportunity could make social life fluid to the point of decomposing it and, with money as the main motive of action, the poison of inequality had been introduced everywhere. A balanced society would impose burdens and risks proportionate to the power and well-being of individuals: an employer who was guilty of an offense against an employee ought to be made to suffer far more than an employee guilty of an offense against an employer. Equally at variance with contemporary opinion was her view that publications destined to influence public opinions about the conduct of life should not be permitted to deny the eternal obligations towards human beings once these had been solemnly recognized by law. The entire daily and weekly press, as well as reviews and literature, should be subject to this constraint. Her reason was that she felt attempts to influence opinion to be acts and should be as subject to the law as any other type of act. People had a need for truth—the most sacred of all needs—and were to a large extent in the hands of professional writers and broadcasters. If these members of the press were convicted of intentional falsehood, they should be punished. What Weil was concerned to safeguard was the freedom of the intellect to which she felt modern techniques of propaganda and advertisement were radically hostile. Underlying all these suggestions was her unwillingness to consider political institutions, however democratic, as the main legitimizers of the distribution of power, her awareness of the danger of all collective activity, and her insistence that genuine liberty and equality could only be founded by reference to other-worldly values.

Particularly striking is Weil's critique of the doctrine of natural rights. In what is perhaps her most famous essay, *On Human Personality*,[10] she denied the idea of rights as fundamental to social organization—and thus put in question the mainstream of Western political thought from the founding of the United States to the Charter of the United Nations. For Weil, any political theory that took the concept of human rights as its foundation was misguided. Rights were, for her, "linked with the notion of sharing out, of exchange, of measured quantity. It has a commercial flavour, essentially evocative of legal claims and arguments. Rights are always asserted in a tone of contention; and when this tone is adopted, it must rely upon force in the background, or else it will be laughed at." The true foundation of political theory was the concept of obligation since "the notion of obligations comes before that of rights, which is subordinate and relative to the former." This was because an obligation would lose none of its force if it went unrecognized—whereas an unrecognizable right was a worthless article. With this rejection of rights as a starting-point, she launched an attack on the idea of the person as a proprietor of these rights. This attack was prompted, in part, by the contemporary personalism of Emmanuel Mounier and the centrality accorded to the concept of the person in the political thought of Jacques Maritain. However, both of these thinkers give a quite different sense to the word "person" from that adopted by Weil. For her, the contemporary Faustian aspirations to self-development, the insistence on the right to satisfy one's desires, the cultivation of individual personality were all mistaken. Truth and beauty were essentially impersonal. The great achievements of humanity such as the *Iliad,* Greek geometry, Gregorian chant, Romanesque architecture were not the product of personal desire. In mathematics it was the varied mistakes that reflected the individual personalities, not the single correct answer. For Weil, the person was everything that said "I," whereas "the whole effort of the mystics has been to become such that there is no part left in their soul to say 'I.'" Taken in this sense, the person is that part of the human being which nurtures pride, egoism, and notoriety. Weil added immediately that "the part of the soul which says 'we' is infinitely more dangerous still": human beings could not get rid of the narrowness of their persons by sinking them in some sort of collectivity with all the dangers of idolatry and totalitarianism that this implied. There was however a close connection between the two in that the cult of the person led to social conditioning and to subordination of the individual to the collective. Note again how Weil almost deduces her politics from her metaphysics. Since God, Truth, Beauty and so on are impersonal it follows that they cannot be reached by the personal in human beings. The current political correlate of this relationship is the collective.

This rejection of personalism forms the basis of Weil's questioning of the notion of right as a possible foundation for political society. She saw in rights little more than a mechanism for bargaining that depended for its validity on the person claiming the rights having the force to implement the claim. Weil did not wish to reject the whole concept of rights, but she did insist that they could only be effective in a society which had achieved a real equality based on obligation and need. The idea of obligation was more fundamental than that of right: "Rights are always found to be related to certain conditions. Obligations alone remain independent of conditions. They belong to a realm situated above all conditions, since it is situated above this world." In Weil's opinion, any attempt to construct a social and political culture without reference to eternal values was bound to lead to confusion, a confusion only compounded by the attempt to interpret rights themselves as absolute principles. The obvious weakness of utilitarianism as an overarching theory has recently led to revival of the language of rights in the hands of such subtle writers as John Rawls or Ronald Dworkin. But, according to Weil, the concept of right is subordinate and will not bear the burden placed upon it in much contemporary political thought. The language of rights was already informed by those who had power. Such language would be, and was, misused. Therefore it could not be wholly good and had to be subordinate to language which tried to convey those goods which, being supernatural, were eternal. Weil's constant reference here is to "another world." As she says: "It is only what comes from heaven that can make a real impress on the earth." Politics is thus deprived of its autonomy in that the person gives way to the impersonal and rights give way to obligations which have their source outside the political.

Although this talk of "other world" might sound rather ethereal, her negative view of rights was formulated in the context of an attempt to formulate fairly specific proposals for a post-war constitution. Given her strictures on the impoverishment of contemporary political culture, it will come as no surprise that all of Weil's proposals were premised on the view that any satisfactory renewal of society depended on a restoration of the centrality of religion as a companion and complement to scientific education. Stupid doctrines about miracles and divine Providence had only enhanced the opposition between religion and a science left almost entirely to its own devices. The solution was not to be found in relegating religion to a "private" affair, since that would simply compound the difficulty. What Weil wanted to do was to rethink all aspects of society in terms of religion in its basic sense of the production of meaning by linking all aspects of life to an Absolute. But this did not mean subjecting society to some sort of religious control. The corrupting influence of Rome on Christianity had already shown what sort of noxious fruits such an approach yielded. The problem was to rediscover a sense of the sacred, not as something separate but as an atmosphere bathing the whole of society, which it enlightened but did not dominate. Such a religion was entirely compatible with science, whose true definition was "the study of the beauty of the world." Fundamentally, the objects of religion and of science were identical: the unity of the established order of the universe. "It is one and the same thing, which with respect to God is eternal Wisdom; with respect to the universe, perfect obedience; with respect to our love, beauty; with respect to our intelligence, balance of necessary relations; with respect to our flesh, brute force."[11] Scientific investigation, therefore, was only one form of religious contemplation and not the uncontrolled and ultimately meaningless drive that dominated a contemporary society which suffered from a surfeit of means and a dearth of ends.

It is interesting for our purposes to compare Weil's proposals in *The Need for Roots* with her "sketch of a free society" in *Oppression and Liberty* written in 1934 before her conversion experiences. In her earlier work the ideal basis for society had been "a form of material existence wherein only efforts exclusively directed by a clear intelligence would take place, which would imply that each worker himself had to control, without referring to any external rule, not only the adaptation of his efforts to the piece of work to be produced, but also their co-ordination with the efforts of all the other members of the collectivity."[12] Her central image of modern society was a production line with workers producing automatically under the constant surveillance of a foreman. The image of her free collectivity is that of a handful of building workers confronted by a particular problem, each thinking of possible solutions and suggesting them to the others, and then the group unanimously adopting the method conceived by one of them who may or may not have had any official authority over the rest. Rousseau's idea of the general will, reinterpreted in a severely intellectualist and individualist manner, is extended to cover all aspects of socio-economic life.

While in the 1940s Weil shows no diminution of interest in social and political questions (her last essay was on Marxism), the constant emphasis on the supernatural gives her later writings a different tone. In *The Need for Roots* she follows *Oppression and Liberty* in being concerned with an order that will not fall victim to totalitarianism. She is still opposing any centralized state power, still advocating a strong liberty of choice with as few laws as possible, and still utopian in the sense of proposing measures whose realization she did not think immediately possible. But her ideal society is no longer based on the enlightened good-will of individuals but on contact with the supernatural and divine grace. These changes are accompanied by a shift in her attitude to the collective. In *Oppression and Liberty* (and in her later *Notebooks*) collectivities in general had been the object of her implacable polemic. At the beginning of *The Need for Roots*, however, she writes that "we owe our respect to a collectivity, of whatever kind—country, family, or any other—not for itself but because it is food for a certain number of human souls" and that "the degree of respect owing to human collectivities is a very high one...."[13] What she has primarily in mind here is a person's "country" as the matrix of society's identity and as the guardian of its traditions and values across generations. She is concerned here to delineate a more genuine form of patriotism. This patriotism should be based on one's country as a source of rootedness. Weil's hostility, previously directed at collectivities, is now directed at the state.[14] Thus whereas her pre-war writings were based on a profound dissatisfaction with any sort of politics, her new religious perspective allows her to adopt an attitude that gives meaning and hope to political activity.

Some commentators—particularly Conor Cruise O'Brien—have characterized Weil's later writings as profoundly antipolitical. It is true that in some of her more mystical writings she speaks derogatively of earthly arrangements: "The city gives us the feeling of being at home. We must take the feeling of being at home into exile. We must be rooted in the absence of a place." However, in *The Need for Roots* and the accompanying paper and proposals written for the Free French, Weil demonstrates her enduring concern for the human and the political. Those who accuse her of being antipolitical have in mind such of her proposals as the banning of political parties. These commentators see politics as essentially concerned with difference, argument, strife. In principle this accusation is misplaced: Weil's proposals are not intended to eliminate differences, but to make sure that differences of opinion were based on accurate information and an appropriate approach to politics in general. Weil does not oppose the formation of political associations: it is their corruption in the Third Republic and the lack of any genuine patriotism that has made the idea of democracy an object of derision. She saw the functionalism and conformity of party politics together with the corrupting influence of an uncontrolled mass media as inherently hostile to truth and as undermining the bases of any genuine opinion formation. Whether, in any readily conceivable practice, her proposals would avoid lapsing into authoritarian government is, of course, doubtful.

But whatever may be the practical consequences of Weil's views, the point to be emphasized here is the way in which Weil's later politics is informed by a Platonic metaphysics. Her view of the superiority of obligations over rights is based on the assertion that rights are always relative to specific conditions and therefore inferior to obligations which, since they had their origin in a realm above the world, are independent of, and superior to, all conditions. Her metaphysical claim, therefore, is that "there is a reality outside the world, that is to say, outside space and time, outside man's mental universe, outside any sphere whatsoever that is accessible to human faculties. Corresponding to this reality, at the center of the human heart, is the longing for an absolute good, a longing which is always there and is never appeased by any object in this world."[15] From this fact followed the conclusion that "there is no guarantee for democracy, or for the protection of the person against the collectivity, without a disposition of public life relating it to the higher good which is impersonal and unrelated to any political form."[16] The centrality that Weil accords to the supernatural is no escapism but a necessary condition for a decent life in the here and now.

The inescapable human longing for absolute good was in constant danger of misdirection. Such misdirection was the origin of totalitarianism, against which the only defense was the allocation to religion of its rightful place in society. To relegate religion to a private affair in a secular society was no solution, although it was in keeping with the spirit of an age which regarded religion as a matter of choice, opinion, taste, or even caprice, something like the choice of a political party or even a tie. Weil's rehearsal of the disastrous effects of the contemporary separation of sacred and profane, public and private did not mean that she wished to see the return of an "official" religion or the establishment of any church. The

suspicion with which she viewed the church was similar to
that with which she viewed the state. Choice, consent, and
freedom of conscience were essential to Weil who was, and
always remained, a supreme individualist. But she wished to
see this individualism combined with a sense of public space
typical of the political philosophy of her beloved Greeks and
more recently elaborated by such thinkers as Hannah Arendt
or Alasdair MacIntyre.[17] The role of the state here was not to
impose any religion through its political power but, as in the
conception of Aristotle, to constitute the arena where meaningful debate could turn a human community into a genuine
"city." The modern penchant for privatization not only
affected religion: justice and truth were also its casualties and
the resulting lack of legitimacy opened the way to totalitarianism. If religion did not occupy its rightful place, then politics would expand to fulfill its function and the result would
be idolatry. Only God could legitimately be considered as an
end in Himself. In today's uprooted culture, "the first consequence, equally affecting all spheres, is generally that, relations being cut, each thing is looked upon as an end in itself.
Uprooting breeds idolatry."[18] It was not just the expulsion of
religion from public life that endangered the present age:
conceptions of God, such as any idea of Providence, of God's
being active in the world, was equally menacing. Weil had in
mind here certain aspects of ancient Israel, Rome, and even
Christianity itself: "Christendom became totalitarian, con-
quering, exterminating when it failed to develop the idea of
the absence and non-action of God here below."[19] In effect,
Weil is advocating an apophatic approach to politics. Her
indications of what might constitute a true civilization are all
negative, condemning the idolatry of money, a degraded conception of justice, the absence of religious inspiration, false
ideas of greatness, etc. In her conception, the role of politics
is to clear as much space as possible for the contemplation of
God. And true religion has nothing to say to politics except
that it should never try to usurp the place of religion and pre-
tend to be an end in itself.

Notes

1. M. Veto, *La Metaphysique religieuse de Simone Weil* (Paris: 1971), 148.

2. S. Weil, *The Need for Roots* (New York: Routledge, 1952), 41.

3. Ibid., 109.

4. Ibid., 115.

5. Ibid., 255.

6. Cf. F. Rosen, "Labor and Liberty: Simone Weil and the Human Condition," *Theoria and Theory* 7 (1973): 33.

7. Weil, *Need for Roots*, 209.

8. S. Weil, *Ecrits de Londres* (Paris: Gallimard, 1957), 89.

9. Weil, *Need for Roots*, 15.

10. S. Weil, *On Human Personality*, reprinted in *Simone Weil: An Anthology*, ed. S. Miles (London: Virago, 1986), 69–98, from which the following quotations are taken.

11. Weil, *Need for Roots*, 281.

12. S. Weil, *Oppression and Liberty* (London: Routledge, 1958), 98.

13. Weil, *Need for Roots*, 7.

14. See further M. Dietz, *Between the Human and the Divine: The Political Thought of Simone Weil* (Totowa, N.J.: Rowan and Littlefield, 1988), 151.

15. *Simone Weil: An Anthology*, 221.

16. Ibid., 97.

17. See e.g. H. Arendt, *The Human Condition* (Chicago: University of Chicago Press, 1970); MacIntyre, *Whose Justice? Which Rationality?*

18. Weil, *Need for Roots*, 65.

19. S. Weil, *Cahiers* (Paris: Plon, 1970), vol. 3, p. 141.

Further Reading

Blum, Larry and Vic Seidler. *A Truer Liberty: Simone Weil and Marxism.* London: Routledge, 1990.

Coles, Robert. *Simone Weil: A Modern Pilgrimage.* New York: Addison-Wesley, 1987.

Dietz, Mary. *Between the Human and the Divine: The Political Thought of Simone Weil.* Totowa, N.J.: Rowman and Littlefield, 1988.

Hellman, John. *Simone Weil: An Introduction to Her Thought.* Waterloo, Ont.: Wilfrid Laurier University Press, 1982.

Little, J. P. *Simone Weil: Waiting on Truth.* New York: Berg, 1988.

McLellan, David. *Utopian Pessimist: The Life and Thought of Simone Weil.* New York: Simon and Schuster, 1990.

Nevin, Thomas. *Simone Weil.* Chapel Hill, N.C.: University of North Carolina Press, 1991.

Petrement, Simone. *Simone Weil: A Life.* New York: Pantheon, 1976.

Pierce, Roy. *Contemporary French Political Thought.* New York: Oxford University Press, 1966.

Weil, Simone. *Oppression and Liberty.* Amherst, Mass.: University of Massachusetts Press, 1973.

———. *The Need for Roots.* Boston: Routledge, 1978.

White, George. *Simone Weil: Interperetations of a Life.* Amherst, Mass.: University of Massachusetts Press, 1981.

3
Liberal Politics:
Reinhold Niebuhr

Only those with no sense of the profundities of history
could deny that various nations and classes, various social
groups and races are at various times placed in such a
position that a special measure of the divine mission in
history falls upon them. In that sense God has chosen us
in this fateful period of world history.

Reinhold Niebuhr

During his long life, Niebuhr was a consistently prolific
writer. Like many, he was politically more radical in his youth
than in his later years. In order, therefore, to show the connection between Christianity and politics in his work, I shall
discuss first a striking example of his earlier work before
going on to that of his maturity. This will show to what extent
his religious conceptions changed in line with his political
ideas.

Reinhold Niebuhr was born in Wright City, Missouri, in
1892. His mother was a preacher's daughter and his father a
minister of the German Evangelical Synod. After graduating
from the Eden Seminary, which was the denominational
seminary for the Synod, Niebuhr spent two years at the Yale
Divinity School before becoming pastor of the Bethel Evangelical Church in Detroit where he stayed for thirteen years.
During his time in Detroit Niebuhr was heavily engaged in
political activism on behalf of left-wing causes, developed

close ties with trade unions, and was a member of the Socialist Party. In 1928 Niebuhr was appointed to a professorship
of Christian Ethics at Union Theological Seminary in New
York City, an association which remained for the rest of his
life. During the 1930s and 1940s Niebuhr produced a stream
of widely read books linking Christianity with contemporary
problems. At the same time, he gradually abandoned his
socialist commitments, and became a firm supporter of Roosevelt's New Deal. In 1947 he became an advisor to the State
Department's Policy Planning Staff under Marshall. In spite
of a series of illnesses beginning in 1952, Niebuhr continued
to be much sought after by leaders of the Democratic Party,
including John F. Kennedy, and widely acclaimed for the way
he expressed what Schlesinger termed the "vital center" of
American politics. He died in 1971.

Niebuhr has the distinction of being considered by many
to be not only the most important theologian that the United
States has produced this century but its most prominent
political theorist. His reputation as a political theorist rests
on his status as an establishment theologian after World War
II and the fact that a number of influential secular thinkers
and politicians—Kennan, Acheson, Schlesinger—admired
his political wisdom as much as they disregarded his theology. Niebuhr's colleague Hans Morgenthau said of him that
"it is indicative of the very nature of American politics and of
our thinking that it is not a statesman, not a practical politician, let alone a professor of political science or of philosophy, who can claim the distinction of being the greatest living
political philosopher of America."[1] Morgenthau attributed
this position to the lack of self-criticism among Americans of
their political institutions and the need for an outsider, a theologian such as Niebuhr, to offer a critical perspective *sub
specie aeternitatis.* But it is rather the position of religion in
American society that enabled Niebuhr to become such a
prominent political thinker. To see how this prominence is
possible, it is necessary to understand that the equation of
left versus right with secular versus religious is much less

powerful in the United States than it is in Europe. The Puritan tradition has strongly influenced American politics: its covenant theology providing a contractual basis for political obedience, its doctrine of original sin affording guidelines as to how a limited government should be maintained, and its idea of a chosen people conferring on the United States a mission parallel to that of Israel in the Old Testament. In general, religion has provided a profound unifying force in American politics, enabling the nation to agree on certain fundamental political values.

Viewed in such a context, Niebuhr's influence is more readily understood. He was a theologian who got his views from experience. As his biography shows, his pastoral work in Detroit informed his early thinking on social ethics. This was followed by theological work and then a return to more political concerns after World War II. He thus tended to look to theology to confirm insights gained on a more secular level. This illuminates the problem of the coherence of Niebuhr's thought. Some have wondered whether the very diverse interests of Niebuhr have any unifying theme, and, in particular, whether the link between his political views and his theology should not be viewed as more or less contingent. Niebuhr was a thinker whose views tended to be rooted in his practical experience which in turn gave rise to ethical reflection: he looked to theology to interpret his experiences and claimed that they were best understood on the basis of biblical faith. The presupposition of this biblical faith is thus validated in the account it gives of historical and political events and the kind of moral and political attitudes to which it gives rise. Niebuhr's analyses of contemporary problems could, and did, appeal to secular minds who could admire the cogency of these analyses while disregarding their genesis. Niebuhr's forte was the explication of biblical symbolism and the application of it to contemporary problems. This lent a philosophical and theological depth to the ideas of American liberal democracy. Lacking any firm ecclesiastical base himself and with no inclination to work out any doctrine of the church, Niebuhr tended to view the American nation in a quasi-ecclesiastical light. For him the United States was a dynamic spiritual reality with Abraham Lincoln as its greatest theologian. Niebuhr saw it as his responsibility to warn against the idolatrous temptations of power and pride that the very achievements of the United States tended to lay in its path. And with a versatility that is virtually precluded by current specialization in divinity schools, Niebuhr could become, with Paul Tillich, America's last and most influential public theologian.

Undoubtedly the major work of Niebuhr's early years is *Moral Man and Immoral Society* published in 1932. The background to this book is the thirteen years Niebuhr spent as a pastor in Detroit and it contains, among other things, a powerfully negative assessment of the promised land that Henry Ford claimed to be creating there. The basic thesis of the book, as indicated by the title, is that "A sharp distinction must be drawn between the moral and social behaviour of individuals and of social groups, national, racial, and economic; and that this distinction justifies and necessitates political policies which a purely individualistic ethic must always find embarrassing."[2] Niebuhr's more specific target is the optimistic and idealist liberal Protestantism that held sway in the 1920s. He writes: "In spite of the disillusionment of the World War, the average liberal Protestant Christian is still convinced that the Kingdom of God is gradually approaching, that the League of Nations is its partial fulfillment and that the Kellogg Pact its covenant, that the wealthy will be persuaded by the Church to dedicate their power and privilege to the common good and that they are doing so in increasing numbers, that the conversion of new individuals is the only safe method of solving the social problem, and that such ethical weaknesses as religion still betrays are due to its theological obscurantism which will be sloughed off by the progress of enlightenment."[3] In sharp contrast to this rosy view of many of his colleagues, Niebuhr provides an assessment of contemporary industrial society which, while consistently softer, recalls that of Simone Weil in *Oppression and Liberty* published only two years later. There is the same emphasis on the self-interested exercise of power, rather than reason, as the underlying social reality, the same view of "the brutal character of the behaviour of all human collectivities,"[4] and the same skepticism about progress. Here Niebuhr is more influenced by the still medieval pessimism of Luther about the possibilities of social change rather than the more forward-looking activism of the Calvinist tradition.

Niebuhr's main target was the optimistic Enlightenment view that the growth of human intelligence and technological capacity would eliminate social injustice. In his view, however, the reality was that those in power in society continued to take for themselves just as much as that power could command. The rise of modern democracy, while curtailing political power, has meant that the more important economic power can exercise itself virtually unchecked. Religion has few resources to stop this ceaseless struggle for power. Instead religion itself degenerates into an asocial quest for the absolute as the religiously sensitive soul despairs of society. The Christian cross is the unconscious glorification of an individual moral ideal, not the symbol of love triumphant in the social world. The growing internationalization of the world only makes things worse. For, while individuals are both selfish and unselfish, nations are inevitably egoistic and can harness the self-sacrificial motives of their citizens to further national ambitions.

If the economically powerful are inevitably hypocritical, are moral resources to be found in their opponents? Like Simone Weil, Niebuhr appreciated Marxism for its grimly realistic and unblinkered analysis of social and economic conflict. Like her, he was skeptical of Marxism's oscillation between moral idealism and its determinist faith in history as bringing the solution to society's problems. Niebuhr's view is that "only the Marxist proletarian" has seen with perfect clarity that one cannot bring about social justice without eliminating the causes of injustice. This same Marxian proletarian, "if he makes mistakes in choosing the means of accomplishing his ends, he has made no mistake either in stating the rational goal toward which society must move, the goal of equal justice, or in understanding the economic foundations of justice. If his cynicism in the choice of means is at times the basis of his undoing, his realism in implementing ethical ideals with political and economic methods is the reason for his social significance."[5] This cynical faith in an unqualified determinism is simply the reflection of the amoral mechanisms of contemporary technological civilization. Marxism was a secular religion: the Marxian view that justice "will be established because weakness will be made strong through economic forces operating with inexorable logic in human history"[6] is more an apocalyptic vision than any science of history. Thus Niebuhr shares with liberation theology an appreciation of Marxism as the best form of social analysis available and for siding with the oppressed since they are those with the clearest view of social reality. In a careful discussion of violence he comes to the conclusion (also echoed in liberation theology) that emancipatory force is in a different moral category from that used to perpetuate domination since "it is important to insist that equality is a higher goal than peace."[7]

Ultimately, however, Niebuhr begins to part company from both Weil and liberation theology in two respects. First, his theory of human nature tends to counterpose the individual to society and ends up as distinctly utilitarian. This is because, second, he maintains that "the religious ideal in its purest form has nothing to do with problems of social justice" and that therefore "it would seem better to accept a frank dualism in morals than to attempt a harmony between the two methods which threatens the effectiveness of both."[8] This dualism was to be a persistent theme in his thought. It led to a pragmatic approach to politics. By proposing policies which "work," pragmatists presuppose a social consensus on values and goals. What works within one such framework will not work within another. In this respect, at least, Niebuhr remained true to the earlier proponents of a social gospel: his task was to elaborate an ethic which would enable Christians to serve American society. As far as practical action was concerned, a Christian ethic coincided with the best in the American political tradition.

Niebuhr characterized his position at the time of writing *Moral Man and Immoral Society* as religiously conservative and politically radical. In fact, his treatment of religion is not particularly conservative in that his connection of religion with a sense of the absolute is reminiscent of Schleiermacher and even of Feurbach. Indeed, there is very little theology in *Moral Man and Immoral Society.* It is true, nevertheless, that as Niebuhr turned his attention more to specifically theological topics his political outlook did move further to the right. In the early 1930s, Niebuhr had advocated a kind of democratic socialism legitimated by Christianity as a "third way" between capitalism and communism. In the 1940s, however, this option disappeared and Niebuhr became as staunchly anti-communist as he was pro-capitalist. Always a strong critic of utopian thought, Niebuhr moved from attacking utopian elements in inter-war liberal progressive theology to exposing what he saw as the utopian drive of contemporary communism. The theological background to this evolution from a socialist to a more Burkean view of society is provided in his *magnum opus* on *The Nature and Destiny of Man*, the Gifford Lectures delivered in Edinburgh at the beginning of the Second World War. In the first volume Niebuhr offers an account of human nature central to which are the ideas of anxiety and pride. Human beings are anxious in virtue of their being created. "Man," says Niebuhr, following Kierkegaard, "being both free and bound, both limited and limitless, is anxious. Anxiety is the inevitable concomitant of the paradox of freedom and finiteness in which man is involved. Anxiety is the internal precondition of sin. It is the inevitable spiritual state of man, standing in the paradoxical situation of freedom and finiteness."[9] Human beings are constantly tempted to respond to this anxiety with the sin of pride when they try to raise their contingent and dependent existence to a status which has unconditional significance—whether through aspiration to unlimited power, or through the illusion of possessing some sort of absolute truth, or through an equally illusory pretense of self-righteousness.[10]

This idolatry of self, which is the major component of sin, is best interpreted and overcome through the myths of the Christian religion. Niebuhr had been much struck in his critique of Marxism by the way it functioned as a religious myth, and this led him to lengthy considerations of the very different Christian myths. A myth conveys a transcendent vision of the whole of history while at the same time illuminating particular events. *The Nature and Destiny of Man* is constructed around the myths of Creation, Fall, Atonement, and Parousia. The validity of these myths is to be measured by the extent to which they clarify our deepest feelings. The first two refer to the problems of anxiety and of pride while the third, and most important, Atonement, shows us the solution. The myth shows us, first, that God has a resource of mercy beyond His justice but that this mercy can only become effective by His taking upon Himself the consequences of His own wrath which is "the world in its essential structure reacting against the sinful corruptions of that structure."[11] Second, it provides the power for the individual to shatter and reconstitute its own self. God's grace is seen here not as something which, in the traditional Catholic view, perfects nature and constitutes the power of God within humanity but as something which acts as a power of forgiveness set over against humanity. For Niebuhr, this was a truth rediscovered by the Reformation but then obscured immediately by the Renaissance with its over-optimistic confidence in human capacities. The Renaissance eclipsed the Reformation because the vast expansion of human knowledge and capabilities consequent of that time enabled the following centuries to combine the biblical idea of sanctification and the fulfillment of life within a meaningful history with an unbounded confidence in human capacities. To this optimism contemporary liberal Protestantism and its neglect of the notion of eschatological judgment has merely given a Christian tinge.

In his later works, however, Niebuhr is clear that the kingdom of God is best approximated by the forms of political organization evolved by Western democracies. Political organization has to maintain a proper trade-off between the power of central government and the powers of various social forces. These two elements of organizing power and of the balance of power will always be in tension with what Niebuhr calls "brotherhood"—let alone the kingdom of God. This political paradox is analogous to the more general paradoxical relationship of history to God's kingdom: "History moves towards the realization of the Kingdom, but yet the judgment of God is upon every new realization."[12] History has moved towards the kingdom with the advent of modern democracy since "Modern democracies tend towards a more equal justice partly because they have divorced political power from special social functions. They endowed all men with a measure of it by giving them the right to review the policies of their leaders. This democratic principle does not obviate the formation of oligarchies in society; but it places a check upon their formation, and upon the exercise of their power."[13] Niebuhr denies, of course, that the social process could be described as the simple progressive triumph of reason over force. He insists that the development of prophetic religion helped to destroy priestly-military oligarchies and create democratic societies. But even here "The achievements of democracy have been tortuously worked out in human history partly because various schools of religious and political thought had great difficulty in fully comprehending the perils to justice in either one or the other instrument of justice—the organization of power and the balance of power."[14] This was because the Christian tradition itself seldom managed to articulate in a form that could give useful political guidance the biblical dialectic between the divine authority of government and its subjection to divine judgment. The most successful

attempt was the later, moderate Calvinism as exemplified in
the constitutionalism of Madison. The conclusion of *The
Nature and Destiny of Man*, that the social and political organizations developed in the West were those most analogous
to the Christian view of history as revealed in the myth of the
Atonement, is continued in *The Children of Light and the
Children of Darkness*. This short book, published in 1944,
applied the broad thesis of *The Nature and Destiny of Man*
to the contemporary political scene marked by the Bretton
Woods agreement and inspired by hopes for the emerging
post-war international order. The idealistic children of light,
liberal and Marxist alike, have not been able to prevent the
children of darkness, who better understood the power of
self-interest, from perverting liberal and socialist ideals for
their own ends. The children of light must become as
worldly-wise as the children of darkness by creating a political system incorporating the twin principles of order and balance in politics, economic and international relations. Given
the gulf between nature and grace, the most to be hoped for
was a pluralist democracy.

Thus Niebuhr firmly rejects the Catholic conception of
natural law as resting on an untenable faith in the purity of
reason and "merely another of the many efforts which men
make to find a vantage point of the unconditioned in history."[15] Here he remained true to the Reformation view that
such an enterprise was vitiated by the corruption of human
nature. Yet it could be argued that this separation of grace
from nature leaves Niebuhr's own social, political, and historical ideas remarkably unanchored in his religious conceptions. But rather it is his very approach to religion which
allows his discussion of secular matters to float free. Like
Simone Weil, though for very different metaphysical reasons,
he is skeptical about notions of moral progress in history.[16]
This is due to the lack of any real historical dimension to his
work. His history is a history of ideas illuminated by biblical
interpretation since "the Bible contains the history, and cul-
mination in Christ, of that *Heilsgeschichte* in which the

whole human enterprise becomes fully conscious of its limits, of its transgressions of those limits, and of the divine answer to its problems."[17] By the same token, his thought is highly individualistic. He has little doctrine of the church as a community of believers and little feel for institutions in general. Even his individual, far from being a universal type, is "an active, dynamic 'self', driven by anxiety, but also capable of a high level of personal integration—perhaps a model of the successful urban American of his day."[18] The result is that Niebuhr's central ethical approach is a sensible utilitarianism. In Weber's terms it is an ethic of social responsibility rather than conscience, and one which thinks in terms of pragmatism and realism. This commonsensical approach which tends to go straight down the center between opposing demands might seem a long way from the ethic of the New Testament. Indeed, "the ethical demands of Jesus are incapable of fulfillment in the present existence of man. They proceed from a transcendent and divine unity of essential reality, and their final fulfillment is possible only when God transmutes the present chaos of this world into its final unity."[19] Since the possibility of a classless society of a Marxian sort (which Niebuhr admitted as an ideal) did not exist, "it is not even right to insist that every action of the Christian must conform to *agape*, rather than to the norms of relative justice and mutual love by which life is maintained and conflicting interests are arbitrated in history."[20] The result was a profound historical pessimism. Niebuhr talked and wrote about the cross but had no theology of the resurrection. The kingdom of God is not a historical possibility so "the final revelation of meaning in history" is vicarious suffering: "It is the vicarious suffering of the representative of God, and not of some force in history, which finally clarifies the obscurities of history and discloses the sovereignty of God over history."[20] Niebuhr was ambivalent as to whether the kingdoms of this earth could approximate to the kingdom of God or whether the latter was in contradiction to the former. Sometimes he wanted to have it both ways: the structures of justice

"invariably contain…both approximations and contradictions
to the ideal of love."[21] But his profound historical pessimism
meant that he tended to see more contradiction than approx-
imation in these structures.

This attitude illustrates the way in which Niebuhr's political ideas were informed by his theology. At first sight,
Niebuhr might seem to be an example of politics being unin-
fluenced by religion: after all, his political thought did appeal
to distinctly secular minds.[23] Nevertheless, although
Niebuhr was severely critical of traditional Lutheranism on
occasion,[24] his own Lutheran background is not without its
effect upon him. The "frank dualism" of his earlier writings is
repeated in a softer version of the Lutheran two kingdoms in
his later work. The emphasis on survival in a sinful world and
the very separation of the kingdom of God from the kingdoms of this earth explains, in part, the ideological fickleness
of Niebuhr as he moves from left to right. His political rec-
ommendations are underdetermined by his theology which
rather provides a spirituality able to sustain a variety of very
different political options. It would be inaccurate to say that
the same theology inspired both the political radical of the
early 1930s and the establishment theologian of the 1950s.
The early writings of Niebuhr contained very little theology:
indeed Niebuhr has been called "a theologian with the theology left out." But when he did turn his attention to theology
it had fairly conservative implications. The later Luther
taught that the Christian ethic was irrelevant to politics in
that "the sayings on mercy belong in God's kingdom and
among Christians, not in the kingdom of the world."[25] In
confining Christian moral precepts to interpersonal relationships, Luther also confined his radical anti-hierarchical,
democratic views to the sphere of religion while assuming
that a political and social hierarchy was both natural and necessary. He wrote that "God has ordained two governments;
the spiritual, by which the Holy Spirit under Christ makes
Christians and pious people, and the secular, which restrains
the unchristian and wicked so that they must needs keep the

peace outwardly, even against their will."[26] In fact, this view
that, since true Christians possessed the kingdom of heaven,
they could leave the kingdom of earth to anyone who wanted
to take it meant that Luther's radical, anti-authoritarian attitude in religion actually served to enhance the secular power.
Luther's failure to appreciate the social and institutional side
of religion, his antipathy to history, and the lack of a future
dimension to his thought all find an echo in Niebuhr's work.

Given these views, it is not surprising that, in social, political, and economic matters, Luther's American followers have
generally been conservative.[27] Niebuhr wrote that, in his
opinion, Luther's legacy contained "The most profound religious insights on ultimate questions of human existence."[28]
From this tradition came Niebuhr's emphasis on the sin of
pride, his individualism, his overly deterministic view of history, and his pessimism about the possible success of any collective human endeavor. And the consequence is a neglect
of social institutions, an unwillingness to contemplate the
changing of structures, and a general disregard for the social
and economic embeddedness of ideas. These views were no
doubt enhanced by Niebuhr's own position as a freelance
"circuit-rider on the college campuses" and his consequent
lack of a pastoral and institutional base. Both his life-style
and his Lutheranism enabled him to produce a theology and
particularly a politics, which, too, was freelance.

Notes

1. H. Morgenthau, "The Influence of Reinhold Niebuhr in American Political Life and Thought," in *Reinhold Niebuhr: A Prophetic Voice in Our Time*, ed. H. Landon (Greenwich: Seabury Press, 1962), 109.

2. R. Niebuhr, *Moral Man and Immoral Society: A Study in Ethics and Politics* (London: SCM Press, 1963), p. x.

3. Ibid., 79.

4. Ibid., p. xx.

5. Ibid., 164.

6. Ibid., 155.

7. Ibid., 165.

8. Ibid., 263, 270.

9. R. Niebuhr, *The Nature and Destiny of Man: A Christian Interpretation* (London: Nisbet, 1941), vol. 1, p. 194.

10. Ibid., vol. 1, p. 198.

11. Ibid., vol. 2, p. 58.

12. Ibid., vol. 2, p. 273.

13. Ibid., vol. 2, p. 273.

14. Ibid., vol. 2, p. 278.

15. Ibid., vol. 2, p. 262.

16. Ibid., vol. 2, p. 254.

17. Ibid., vol. 1, p. 157.

18. D. McCann, *Christian Realism and Liberation Theology: Practical Theologies in Creative Conflict* (Maryknoll: Orbis, 1981), 127.

19. Niebuhr, *Nature and Destiny of Man*, vol. 2, p. 92.

20. R. Niebuhr, *An Interpretation of Christian Ethics* (New York: Harper, 1935), 67.

21. Niebuhr, *Nature and Destiny of Man*, vol. 2, p. 46.

22. Ibid., vol. 2, p. 245.

23. Cf. S. Hauerwas, *Against the Nations* (Notre Dame, Ind.: University of Notre Dame Press, 1992), 33.

24. Cf. Niebuhr, *Nature and Destiny of Man*, vol. 2, p. 192.

25. M. Luther, *Werke* (Weiner Ausgabe), vol. 18, p. 289, as quoted in S. Wolin, "Politics and Religion: Luther's Simplistic Imperative," *American Political Science Review* 50 (1956): 40.

26. Ibid., 38.

27. For survey material, see M. Weber, "Religion and Conservative Social Attitudes," in *Views from the Pews: Christian Beliefs and Attitudes*, ed. R. Johnson (Philadelphia: Fortress, 1983).

28. *Worldview* (June 1973): 14, as quoted in *Reinhold Niebuhr and the Issues of Our Time*, ed. R. Harries (London: Mowbrays, 1986).

Further Reading

Brown, Robert. Ed. *The Essential Reinhold Niebuhr: Selected Essays and Addresses*. New Haven, Conn.: Yale University Press, 1986.

Durkin, Kenneth. *Reinhold Niebuhr*. London: Chapman, 1989.

Fox, Richard. *Reinhold Niebuhr*. New York: Pantheon, 1985.

Harries, Richard. Ed. *Reinhold Niebuhr and the Issues of Our Time*. Oxford: Mowbray, 1986.

Keeley, Charles, and Robert Bretall. *Reinhold Niebuhr: His Religious, Political and Social Thought*. New York: Macmillan Press, 1956.

McCann, Dennis. *Christian Realism and Liberation Theology: Practical Theologies in Creative Conflict*. Maryknoll: Orbis, 1981.

Merkley, Paul. *Reinhold Niebuhr: A Political Account*. Montreal and London: McGill-Queen's University Press, 1975.

Niebuhr, Richard H. *The Social Sources of Denominationalism*. New York: Henry Holt, 1929.

Niebuhr, Reinhold. *Moral Man and Immoral Society: A Study in Ethics and Politics*. New York: Scribner, 1932.

———. *The Nature and Destiny of Man: A Christian Interpretation*. 2 vols. New York: Nisbet, 1941 and 1943.

———. *The Children of Light and the Children of Darkness: A Vindication of Democracy and a Critique of its Traditional Defense*. New York: Scribner, 1944.

Scott, Nathan. Ed. *The Legacy of Reinhold Niebuhr*. Chicago: University of Chicago Press, 1975.

Stone, Ronald. *Reinhold Niebuhr: Prophet to Politicians*. Nashville: Abingdon, 1972.

4
Socialist Politics: Liberation Theology

> By keeping historical events in their proper perspective,
> theology helps safeguard society and the Church from
> regarding as permanent what is only temporary. Critical
> reflexion thus plays an inverse role of an ideology which
> rationalizes and justifies a given social and ecclesial order.
> Gustavo Guttiérez

Whereas Simone Weil's Christianity yielded a peculiar
type of conservatism and Niebuhr's Christianity issued, even-
tually, in a modified endorsement of the *status quo*, liberation theology offers an interpretation of Christianity which is
widely associated with left-wing politics, with socialism. How
is the "liberation" of liberation theology distinctive? After all,
there are few Christians who would not endorse the biblical
proposition that "the truth shall set you free." Niebuhr talked
frequently about freedom, and Simone Weil's critique of
contemporary society was intended to liberate people from
false conceptions of greatness, from the idolatry of money,
from the degraded idea of justice. But while Niebuhr's religion is at one remove (at least) from politics and therefore
only indirectly politically prescriptive and Weil proposes the
reorganization of this world in order to enable us to focus
on the world beyond, liberation theology presents us with a
connection between religion and politics at its tightest. The
liberation which this theology finds proclaimed in the Bible

is a liberation primarily of the poor and oppressed. It is a liberation which takes place inside history and involves an over-
throw of the political and economic structures which
perpetuate this oppression. God, in other words, is not some
supernatural mystery above history: she/he is active in history
and is found wherever the poor and underprivileged are
struggling to overcome their oppression.

Liberation theology is a movement with many different
versions and nuances. It is to be found in many different
places: in South Africa and the Philippines, for example, and
even in the advanced industrial conditions of the West where
it has obvious affinities with black and feminist theology. But,
for historical reasons, it is mainly associated with Central and
Latin America. According to Lenin, "only Communism and
Catholicism offer two diverse, complete and inconfusable
conceptions of human life."[1] But he reckoned without the
experience of Latin America which is the only continent to
have been both Christian and colonized. Christian Europe
was never colonized and other colonized continents have
not, on the whole, been Christian. After centuries of domination and oppression, first by Spain and later by the United
States, the increased industrialization and urbanization produced, in the 1930s, populist movements demanding democratic control over social and economic policies. Following
the Second World War, Kennedy's Alliance for Progress and
Christian Democracy in general failed to effect much
improvement. The growing influence of multinational corpo-
rations allied to repressive and unrepresentative ruling
groups led to greater radicalization of opposition, a radicalization helped both by the success of the Cuban revolution
and by the decline in power and cohesion of the traditional
communist parties.

The theology which reflected upon and accompanied this
radicalization was, in its origin in the early 1960s, mainly a
clerical movement of younger theologians whose studies
in Europe had led them to abandon traditional Thomism
in favor of biblical and patristic sources and the "salvation

history" contained therein. They were also influenced, on their own continent, by such works as *Pedagogy of the Oppressed* by the Brazilian educator Paolo Freire and the various polemics of Ivan Illich from the Intercultural Center for Documentation at Cuernavaca in Mexico. The Second Vatican Council (1961–1965) appeared to give official blessing to aspirations for church renewal—a process which reached its Latin American high point in 1968 when the Second Conference of Latin American Bishops meeting at Medellín in Columbia proclaimed its "option for the poor." The countries who have made the biggest contribution to liberation theology are Argentina, Uruguay, Chile, Peru, and Brazil (which has more Catholics than any other country in the world). And it will come as no surprise that, in such a continent-wide movement, there are very diverse currents. Liberation theology is supported by a significant—though definitely minoritarian—part of the Episcopate, including such notable figures as Helder Câmera, Archbishop of Recife in Brazil. Its theologians vary from the Columbian Camillo Torres, who felt he could best fulfill his priestly vocation by joining the guerrillas, was killed by the security forces, and has become something of a martyr of the left, to the decidedly more nuanced writings of the Peruvian Jesuit Gustavo Guttiérez, whose *Theology of Liberation* is the best selling of liberation theology books. The most magisterial writings are the multi-volume works of Juan Luis Segundo.

These rather diverse currents are united by several common themes. The most general is the self-critical, self-reflexive attitude which they all share. Liberation theologians are usually themselves part of the pastoral bureaucracy and thus have experience of the social and political involvement of the institutional church. They are inserted into communities already struggling in one way or another to control their own destinies and a historical and political dimension to their theology is almost inevitable. They are aware at first hand of the involvement of the Latin American church in the social and political structures that have compounded the domination and oppression of the mass of the people. As Guttiérez says: "An awareness of the need for self-liberation is essential to a correct understanding of the liberation process. It is not a matter of 'struggling for others,' which suggests paternalism and reformist objectives, but rather of becoming aware of oneself as not completely fulfilled and as living in an alienated society."[2] This self-critical attitude also rules out any dogmatic interpretation of the Christian faith. The immobility of dogma inevitably serves to sanctify the present order of things, whereas Christian faith is inherently critical and subversive. Although this sounds like, and is, a radical approach, liberation theologians would claim that their method of understanding biblical texts is the traditional one contained in the Bible itself where New Testament authors use Old Testament texts to interpret to themselves and others their own particular situation.[3]

This critical and subversive attitude is found by liberation theology in the biblical texts which they consider to be central to their situation—Exodus, the Prophets, the Beatitudes, Matthew 25, and Jesus' preaching of the kingdom in the gospels. Liberation theology is concerned to reevaluate the place in the Christian canon of the Old Testament to which Christian rebels have traditionally appealed. Unlike Simone Weil who saw the Old Testament, and particularly the Pentateuch, as a repulsive glorification of politico-military success, liberation theology sees the earthy realism of the Old Testament—and particularly the Exodus—as a paradigm of political liberation. According to Guttiérez, "the liberation of Israel is a political action. It is the breaking away from a situation of despoliation and misery and the beginning of the construction of a just and fraternal society."[4] The Exodus from Egypt, a country which was the home of a sacred monarchy, reinforces the idea that faith desacralizes creation: the Exodus is "the desacralisation of social praxis which from that time on will be the work of man."[5] Talking of the Exodus in words that echo the master-slave dialectic of Hegel, Jean Cardonnel states: "The concrete experience of liberation is the only way to discover the fact of creation. It is only the deeply lived experience of oppression that prompts man to work toward his radical liberation, in which process he can come to discover that the world is a creation."[6] Niebuhr also puts at the center of his theology the Jewish prophetic myths of Israel as a yardstick for interpreting all experience. But rather than using the myths of Creation and Fall, as does Niebuhr, to construct a general theory of human nature, liberation theology incorporates these myths into the structure of the Exodus paradigm: "The creation of the world initiates history, the human struggle, and the salvific adventure of Yahweh. Faith in creation does away with its mythical and supernatural character. It is the work of a God who saves and acts in history; since man is the centre of creation, it is integrated into the history which is being built by man's efforts."[7] On this reading, the Exodus and the prophetic writings are the high points of the Old Testament with the royal theology of the Davidic monarchy as an unfortunate interlude.

Turning to the New Testament, liberation theology sees the message of Exodus as ultimately fulfilled through the ministry of Christ the Liberator. The key texts here are the Beatitudes, the preaching of the kingdom by Jesus, and the separation of the sheep from the goats in Matthew 25. And Mary, rather than the adored Virgin of pious devotion, is seen as a leader in a struggle for justice who talked of God's having "put down the mighty from their thrones and exalted those of low degree." Liberation theology is not particularly concerned to link Jesus with the contemporary revolutionary movement of the Zealots nor to picture him as an armed guerrilla fighter, but rather to find in his political Messianism suggestive signs and symbols. On this view, Jesus was indeed engaged in active opposition to established political authority but, at the same time, his message was that the liberation of the Jewish people was only part of a universal revolution with more profound and permanent consequences than could be encompassed by the political liberation of a single people. In all this, liberation theology is seeking to give a social and political dimension to traditional Christian concepts which tended to have become "privatized." For theologians of liberation, the injunction to love your enemy, for example, no longer involves a vague and universal goodwill. In Guttiérez's words: "Love does not mean that oppressors are no longer enemies nor does it eliminate the radicalness of the combat against them. 'Love of enemies' does not ease tensions; rather it challenges the whole system and becomes a subversive formula."[8] Again, "poverty" is not something spiritual or individual, but implies solidarity with the poor and a protest *against* poverty. And salvation is viewed, at least in the first instance, as liberation from specific social and political oppression.[9]

One of the most controversial aspects of liberation theology is its relationship to Marxism. For the Vatican, influenced by its experience in Eastern Europe and the Soviet Union, the matter is fairly clear in that "atheism and the denial of the human person, his liberty and his rights, are at the core of the Marxist theory" and thus, however diverse the currents of contemporary Marxism may be, "to the extent that they remain fully Marxist, these currents continue to be based on certain fundamental tenets which are not compatible with the Christian conception of humanity and society."[10] It is true that liberation theology in general uses a lot of Marxist social analysis, that it has affinities with the humanism of Marx's early writings, and that it insists on the utopian elements in the gospel. Whereas Simone Weil rejected Marxism for its superstitious belief in the principle of progress in the shape of the development of the productive forces and Niebuhr accused it of promoting both cynicism and fanaticism while relying on what were at best half-truths about human nature, liberation theology has on the whole welcomed the critical insights of Marx's dialectical vision.

Marxism is itself, of course, a complex intellectual and political phenomenon: what appears as a potentially liberating doctrine in Brazil appears to be exactly the reverse in, say, Czechoslovakia. The hesitancy of the Vatican, caught in the

middle and subject to pressure from both areas, is under-
standable. Liberation theologians have been accustomed to
separating out three different aspects of Marxism. The first is
Marxism as sociology producing a would-be scientific analysis of society; the second is Marxism as a form of socialism, a
political project for society, a means of confronting a particular period in history and of leading it towards goals that are
partial and subject to revision; the third is Marxism as an
overall philosophy, an all-embracing world view offering an
explanation of the whole of reality. For the Vatican "the ideological principles come prior to the study of social reality and
are presupposed in it. Thus no separation of the parts of this
epistemologically unique complex is possible. If one tries to
take only one part, say, the analysis, one ends up having to
accept the entire ideology."[11] Liberation theologians by contrast think that they can profit much from the first aspect,
give conditional support to the second, while having strong
reservations about the third.

The "dialogue" of Christianity and Marxism has a history
preceding that of liberation theology. In post-war Europe
where most Marxists and some Christians had recently been
united in a struggle against fascism and where Marxism itself
was being reinterpreted through the recent publication of
Marx's early writings, this conversation centered on different
interpretations of the elusive notion of humanism. Oppositional Marxists in Eastern Europe were keen to espouse
humanism as a defense against the oppressive bureaucracies
of state socialism, while the progressive theology of such writers as Bultmann and Tillich defined itself in terms of the currently dominant existentialist version of humanism. In Latin
America, however, the appalling conjunction of political
oppression and economic exploitation meant that this dialogue
between Marxists and Christians took on a different tone from
that in Europe. Whereas in Europe the dialogue was about
general and ultimate questions, the pressing challenges of
Latin America forced the participants to concentrate on
more particular and penultimate problems. At the same

time, humanism itself was in decline, and "man as such" seemed an unreal intellectual construction that should be replaced by reference to identity in terms of gender, class, race, and language—which seemed to preclude Niebuhr's style of reflection on the normative implications of human nature. The influence of structuralism compounded this process which was typified by Sartre's revision of his earlier views and his attempts to come to terms with Marxism which he declared to be "the philosophy of our time." What Aristotle had been to the twelfth and the thirteenth centuries, Marx was to many contemporary theologians of the late twentieth century. As one of the more Marxist-oriented liberation theologians put it in 1974: "Current political theology is opting for a knowledge of historical reality with the same care and attention that scholastic theology paid to the most subtle metaphysical distinctions and that existentialist theology paid to the analysis of depth psychology. Gospel message and political happening serve as principles of mutual interpretation."[12] This "knowledge of historical reality" tended to be mediated through a structuralist reading of Marxism à la Althusser whose critique of the ideological character of humanism was widely influential. The time when Marxism began to have a profound impact on theology was the same time that Althusser's ideas were at their most popular in the Latin countries of Europe and his interpretation of Marx, with its talk of "relatively autonomous levels," etc., explicitly left room (of a sort) for religious belief. The much vaunted "scientificity" of Althusser also made it seem more neutral than other forms of Marxism and more confinable to the first aspect of Marxism mentioned above.

For all that, the links between liberation theology and mainstream Marxist thought are not very precise. Marxism contains certain views that some versions of (thereby impoverished) Christianity have ceased to propagate: of human beings as essentially social, of solidarity with the poor and outcast, of taking history seriously, and of looking towards the future. But these are very broad views and the fact that liberation theologians are certainly anti-capitalist does not make them necessarily Marxist. The most that can be said is that the majority of liberation theologians consider their theology to imply some form of socialism. Their secular political bias could just as well be described as anarchist.[13] The kind of Marxism that the *Instruction* had in mind was clearly that of the Eastern European Communist parties which never had currency among liberation theologians. Indeed, in recent years, they have tended less and less to express themselves in terms borrowed from European Marxism and more in terms that express the interaction of the prophetic tradition of the Bible and the historical experience of Central and Southern America. It is this interaction that gives rise to the two themes that really worry Rome: that the primary location of the church is not in an institution but in the poor and deprived; and that true doctrine is not unchanging but a fruit of experience and action. Ethics and considerations of the kind of relationships obtaining between people are at the very center of liberation theology, rather than being appendages as they are to systematic theology. Hence the priority accorded to ortho*praxy* over ortho*doxy*. If anywhere, it is in this second area that Latin American Christians have used certain aspects of Marxism, with its emphasis on practice and experience to transform their religious heritage. In the words of Bonino, "Perhaps one of the deepest coincidences between a non-dogmatic Marxism and an authentically biblical Christianity lies precisely in this, that both have an absolutely peculiar relation to truth. Both of them demand that their truth be 'verified', that it 'become true', 'that it be fulfilled'. They demand to be confirmed by the facts. They conceive of truth as truth in the facts and it is precisely in this that they stand opposed to all forms of idealism, metaphysics or ideology that understand truth as something 'in itself', outside facts, in a 'separate realm'."[14] Here there is a distinct echo of Marx's *Theses on Feuerbach*, but it is very far from demonstrating any kind of congruence between Christianity and Marxism.

The same point could be expressed in Gramsci's distinction between organic and traditional intellectuals. The liberation

theologians see themselves as organic, as opposed to traditional, intellectuals. Traditional intellectuals (of whom
Niebuhr would be a contemporary example) typically saw
theology as reflecting an eternal wisdom and producing a
kind of rational knowledge which was not contingent on historical events: the theology of traditional intellectuals was
"above" history. The activity of organic intellectuals, by contrast, revolves around an active commitment to a Christian
community: they produce an evolving critical reflection on
society and the church. Theology is thus a second order
activity. It is a reflection on society which, like Hegel's owl of
Minerva, rises only at dusk.

Liberation theology's idea of God is thus radically different from that of Weil and Niebuhr. Weil's conception of God
comes explicitly out of that strand in Christian theology associated with Greek rationalism in which God is conceived of
as unchanging, perfect, impersonal. Faith in such a God
implies doctrine that can be studied, handed down, and pro-
fessed. And this view of God has, not surprisingly, been associated with those advocating, both in church and state,
societies which are institutionalized on clear and well-orga-
nized principles, involving rank and hierarchy. The opposing
strand in Christian theology, with Hebraic rather than Greek
roots, sees God as a personal creator, who acts directly in history. Faith in this God usually involves personal commitment
and is often associated with a voluntarist, egalitarian, and
radical approach to economic, social, and political questions.
In the more classical conception God is omnipotent, omni-
scient, immutable, and, above all, transcendent, as far
removed from the earth as possible, situated, as Weil says,
"the other side of the sky." In Niebuhr, God is a hidden God
who transcends history and acts in a hidden manner that can
at best be only glimpsed by sincere and prayerful individuals.
In liberation theology, by contrast, God's action in history is
manifest—at least to those who ally themselves with the
struggle of the oppressed for liberation.

In Europe and North America belief in God often seems
highly problematic and much thought is given to the question

of God's existence, the problem of evil, the reconciliation of predestination and free will, etc. In Latin America, however, the question is more what sort of God to believe in—a static God or a dynamic God, a God of death or a God of life. The traditional dualism of mind and matter is disregarded and the path to the knowledge of God is seen to lie through human beings. The dialectical vision of liberation theology, therefore, does not concern itself with the timeless attributes of God but reflects on God's own self-description: "I am the Lord your God, who brought you out of the Land of Egypt, out of the house of bondage." Nor does liberation theology spend much time on the traditional questions of how Jesus could be both truly human and truly divine. Whereas in the past it is the divine attributes which have tended to be emphasized with Jesus firmly seated on the right hand of God after his brief visit to earth, liberation theology stresses the fact that Jesus shared the lot of the poor and oppressed and it is there that God is to be found. And given the theme of struggle, it is not surprising that there is more emphasis on the Resurrection than the Crucifixion. The typical political activity associated with liberation theology has been as a catalyst in the formation of Christian base communities. These small groups, of almost Rousseauian inspiration, usually consist in a dozen or more poor families living in the same neighborhood, who meet once or twice a week to reflect on the Bible, understand more fully the social and economic situation surrounding them, and undertake communal projects to change it for the better.[15]

Considering the whole tenor of liberation theology, it is evident that it has close links with politics. Indeed it is often objected that these links are *too* close. How valid are these objections? From a Catholic point of view it sounds distinctly odd. Since at least the time of the Constantinian settlement the Catholic church has in one way or another been continuously involved in politics. To take a recent example, Cardinal Jaime Sin of Manila was widely approved for the active part he played in the downfall of the Marcos regime. The general tenor of church pronouncements, however, is that the church is not wedded to any political system, that its clergy should not engage in political activities, that the church herself as a "ministry of service" is "above" politics, though individual lay members are free to take up what political options they may choose. This attitude springs from a European–North American background of a fairly consensual political system where political parties operate within narrowly agreed parameters and party politics is a choice between competing elites whose policies do not widely differ. In such circumstances, it is obviously not the role of the church to advise its members on whether they should vote Democrat or Republican. Even the United States Catholic Bishops' pastoral letter on *Catholic Social Teaching and the United States Economy* goes no further than advocating a redistributive liberalism as a principle to direct public policy within the current institutional framework.

From the point of view of liberation theology, however, a political struggle to change the inherited institutions is necessary. Whereas traditional theology as done by Niebuhr takes a fairly static and generalized account of individual human experience as its basis, liberation theology substitutes history, and particularly the struggles of oppressed people, as its primary reference point. The God of the liberation theologians is a God who acts as an empowerer of the poor, as their protagonist, who disrupts existing power relations and calls on believers to do likewise. Thus the links between religion and politics here appear at their most intimate. This may, of course, be only an appearance: belief in a God who tells the poor to accept their lot and urges the rich to be charitable towards them also has observable political consequences. Liberation theology appears to have a higher public profile since it is more prescriptive and those who wish to preserve the *status quo* have always seemed less political than those who wished to overturn it. The desire to restrict politics and to compartmentalize it (away from e.g. economics, religion) is one of the hallmarks of the contemporary conservative. From this point of view, politics is an essentially contestable concept.

From another point of view, however, liberation theology is more difficult to fit in to a comparative analysis of the correlation between religion and politics. In the cases of Weil and Niebuhr, the link between their metaphysics and their political prescriptions is clear. Some critics of liberation theology have claimed that it effectively abolishes theology and politicizes religion to such an extent that one of the entities to be correlated virtually disappears. One of the major influences on liberation theology has been the work of Paolo Freire whose *Pedagogy of the Oppressed* advocates a process whereby oppressed people can become critically aware of their situation and transform both society and themselves in a sort of self-creation. This process Freire refers to as "conscientization" and it appears to recognize no external limit on the development of human consciousness. Insofar as it adopts the ideas of Freire, liberation theology rejects the approach of, say, the Integral Humanism of Maritain which distinguished formally between the natural and supernatural ends of humanity, with politics confined to the former as an autonomous but subordinate activity. It even rejects the 'political' theology of Metz which preserves the kingdom of God and the Passion of Christ as elements of a critical negativity that is always set over against the aspirations of humanity. According to its critics, liberation theology takes over the Feuerbachian humanism of the young Marx and thus adopts an ultimately reductive method which deprives it of any theological content. From such a perspective it is difficult to make sense of such central Christian doctrines as the Incarnation. As one of its most percipient critics has put it: "No dialectical *tour de force* can integrate the Epiphany of the Absolute in time with the vision of history as an ongoing struggle of the oppressed to realise the untested feasibility of liberation. This is so because the Incarnation makes God the primary agent or 'Subject' in human history, while the dialectical vision makes it possible for men to enter the historical process as responsible Subjects. If 'history is one' in the sense required by the dialectical vision, then the Incarnation must

be regarded as myth. An enobling and enabling myth perhaps: a symbol of the aspirations of the oppressed for permanent liberation in history; but nevertheless a myth."[16]
Liberation theology is a very diverse phenomenon: this kind
of criticism does seem to apply to the work of theologians
such as Assman who tends to reduce theology to politics,
occasionally to Guttiérez who sometimes confuses them, but
hardly at all to, for example, Segundo. Nevertheless if the
logic of conscientization is pushed far enough, theology itself
is so liberated that it becomes little more than a rhetorical
endorsement of the dialectical vision of a Freire where there
is ultimately no referent outside the all-encompassing libera-
tive practice of humanity.

Notes

1. See J. Hellman, "French 'Left-Catholics' and Communism in the 1930s," *Church History* 45 (1976): 507.

2. G. Guttiérez, *A Theology of Liberation* (Maryknoll: Orbis, 1973), 146.

3. Cf. C. Rowland and M. Corner, *Liberating Exegesis: The Challenge of Liberation Theology to Biblical Studies* (London: SPCK, 1990), 61.

4. Guttiérez, *Theology of Liberation*, 155.

5. Ibid.., 159.

6. J. Cardonnel, *Dieu est mort en Jesus-Christ* (Bordeaux: Centurion, 1968), 123.

7. Guttiérez, *Theology of Liberation*, 154.

8. Ibid, 276.

9. Cf. J. Yoder, *The Politics of Jesus* (Grand Rapids: Eerdmans, 1972) and, more succinctly, H. Roefols, "Liberation Theology: The Recovery of Biblical Radicalism," *American Review of Political Science* 82, no. 2 (June 1988): 554.

10. *Instruction on Certain Aspects of the Theology of Liberation* (Vatican, 1984), 18.

11. Ibid.

12. A. Fierro, *The Militant Gospel: An Analysis of Contemporary Political Theologies* (London: SCM Press, 1977), 106.

13. See L. Damico, *The Anarchist Dimension of Liberation Theology* (New York: Peter Lang, 1987).

14. J. Bonino, *Christians and Marxists: The Mutual Challenge to Revolution* (London: Hodder and Stoughton, 1976), 18.

15. See further L. Boff, *Church: Charisma and Power* (New York: Crossroad, 1985), chap. 9.

16. D. McCann, *Christian Realism and Liberation Theology* (Maryknoll: Orbis, 1981), 184.

Further Reading

Boff, Clodovis. *Theology and Praxis: Epistemological Foundations.* Maryknoll: Orbis, 1987.

Ellis, Marc, and Otto Maduro. *Expanding the View: Gustavo Guttiérez and the Future of Liberation Theology.* Maryknoll: Orbis, 1990.

Fierro, Alfredo. *The Militant Gospel: An Analysis of Contemporary Political Theologies.* London: SCM Press, 1977.

Freire, Paulo. *Pedagogy of the Oppressed.* Harmondsworth: Penguin, 1972.

Gottwald, Norman. *The Tribes of Jahweh: A Sociology of the Religion of Liberated Israel 1250–1050 BCE.* Maryknoll: Orbis, 1979.

Gottwald, Norman. Ed. *The Bible and Liberation: Political and Social Hermeneutics.* Maryknoll: Orbis, 1983.

Guttiérez, Gustavo. *The Truth Shall Make You Free: Confrontations.* Maryknoll: Orbis, 1990.

——. *A Theology of Liberation.* Maryknoll: Orbis, 1973.

——. *The Power of the Poor in History.* London: SCM Press, 1983.

Kee, Alastair. *Marx and the Theology of Liberation.* London: SCM Press, 1990.

Lash, Nicholas. *A Matter of Hope.* London: Darton, Longman and Todd, 1981.

McKellaway, Alexander. *The Freedom of God and Human Liberation.* Philadelphia: Trinity Press, 1990.

McLellan, David. *Marxism and Religion: A Description and Assessment of the Marxist Critique of Christianity.* New York: Harper and Row, 1987.

Pixley, George. *God's Kingdom.* London: SCM Press, 1981.

Rowland, Christopher and Mark Corner. *Liberating Exegesis: The Challenge of Liberation Theology to Biblical Studies.* London: SPCK, 1990.

Segundo, Juan. *The Liberation of Theology.* Dublin: Gill and Macmillan, 1977.

Sobrino, Jon. *The True Church and the Poor.* London: SCM Press, 1985.

Solle, Dorothee. *Political Theology.* Philadelphia: Fortress Press, 1974.

Tabb, William. Ed. *Churches in Struggle: Liberation Theologies and Social Change in North America.* New York: Monthly Review, 1986.

5

Green Politics: Creation Theology

> The new culture will once more have a spiritual dimension, if only because it will be otherwise impossible to break through the vicious circle of material expansion. Without a system of values which from the start is set above the purely economic, this ecological cyclical economy we are striving for cannot come about.
>
> Rudolph Bahro

The final case study of the connection between political principle and religious belief is that of the Green or Environmental movement.[1] The focus here is less sharp since it is the ideas of the movement as a whole that will be discussed rather than those of any individual thinker in particular. Indeed, an initial difficulty might seem to be that, in a sense, all three of the previous lines of thought considered could themselves be seen as "green." Simone Weil felt that the beauty of the natural world mirrored, in its harsh necessity, her own impersonal God and that its "beauty touches us all the more keenly where necessity appears in a most manifest manner, for example in the folds that gravity has impressed upon the mountains, on the waves of the sea, or on the course of the stars."[2] In Reinhold Niebuhr's theology, it has been claimed, is to be found a better understanding of environmental ethics and a more effective strategy for action than in much of traditional Christian thought.[3] And even liberation

71

theology, although more concerned with human ecology, breaks down the dichotomy between spiritual values and material needs with a more holistic understanding of the universe. And yet all three currents have very different religious outlooks.

This difficulty is more apparent than real in that neither Weil nor Niebuhr nor the average liberation theologian places the relation of humanity to nature at the center of their political concerns. And while the spectrum of green thought is very wide—from the light green attempts to persuade consumers to buy in a more environmentally sensitive manner to dark green proposals for a total restructuring of society—a conviction that the central issue facing contemporary society is that of our relation to the natural world is a minimum condition for being considered green. At the same time, this minimum condition is so wide that it is difficult to see what *political* prescription it involves—a point to which we will return later.[4] Indeed, one of the claims of the Green movement is that it transcends the increasingly irrelevant categories of contemporary politics. The very novelty of its outlook means that positive connections between Green politics and religion are, as yet, only tentative.

The negative connections between Green politics and traditional Christianity are, by contrast, much clearer in that a strong theme in much ecological writing has been the responsibility of the Judeo-Christian tradition for a good portion of the destructive attitude to nature that now threatens us all with catastrophe. In 1967 Lynn White published what was to become a much-discussed article entitled "The Historical Roots of our Ecological Crisis"[5] in which he claimed that by destroying pagan animism Christianity had made it possible to exploit nature in a mood of indifference to any intrinsic value that natural objects might contain. Therefore, Christianity bore a huge burden of guilt in encouraging the birth of science and technology, the conjunction of which had given to humanity powers that, to judge by their ecological effects, were out of control. His conclusion was that "we shall continue to have a worsening ecologic crisis until we reject the Christian axiom that nature has no reason for existence save to serve man."[6] Thus White can be seen as extending the link that Weber tried to establish between Protestantism and capitalism to that between Christianity and nature as a whole. And perhaps that link should be seen, in White's case as in Weber's, as a functional rather than a directly causal relationship.

Those who sympathized with White's point of view could find passages in the Old Testament to support their contentions, particularly Genesis, chapter 1, verse 28: "Be fruitful and multiply and replenish the earth and subdue it: and have dominion over the fish of the sea, over the fowl of the air, and over every living thing that moveth upon the earth." This "dominion" view that the role of nature is that of an assemblage of objects to be dominated and used by humanity is reiterated even more strongly in God's words to Noah after the flood (Genesis 9:2-3) and emphasized by the fact that whereas Adam in the Garden of Eden had been a vegetarian, Noah and his descendants were encouraged to be carnivorous. On the other hand, it could be pointed out that this portrait of Adam as having a God-given right to act as a despot towards nature is at variance with the alternative account of creation in Genesis, chapter 2, where Adam is put in the garden "to till it and keep it"—to serve and preserve the earth.[7] Genesis also refers to nature as beautiful, as blessed by God, and, in turn, praising God. In this context, humanity's "dominion" over nature is a call to act as the responsible representative of God's cosmic sovereignty. The covenant made with Noah (Genesis 2:9-14) is a covenant made with every creature—and references to such a covenant with the non-human world are frequently repeated in the Prophets. The New Testament does not have much to say on this topic, although natural objects occupy a prominent role in the parables of Jesus and he compares the lilies of the field favorably to Solomon.

But White's point was not to contribute to the rather specialist and tricky subject of biblical exegesis but to examine

what use the Christian tradition had made of these sacred
texts. Here there is much force in his claim that "not only
modern technology but also the unhesitatingly exploitative
approach to nature that has characterised our culture are
largely reflections of value structures emerging from the
matrix of Latin Christianity."[8] He supports this claim with
impressive examples of the way in which medieval Latin
Christianity encouraged emerging technologies. The argument here would be that the despotic attitude to nature did
not come so much from the Old Testament or even Christianity itself as from the incorporation into Christian doctrine
of the Greek view as articulated by Aristotle and the Stoics.
This view is that nature was created for humankind and that
human beings are *imago dei* insofar as they are rational—
rationality being the key trait which separates humans from
non-humans. This view really came to the fore with the Pela-
gian humanism of Descartes and his followers. It was
Descartes's aim to "find a practical philosophy by means of
which, knowing the force and the action of fire, water, air, the
stars, heaven and all the other bodies which environ us, as
distinctly as we know the different crafts of our artisans, we
can in the same way employ them in all those uses to which
they are adapted, and thus render ourselves the masters and
possessors of nature."[9] A despotic attitude is certainly present in this interpretation of dominion over nature. Such an
attitude becomes even more evident when considering
Descartes's attitude to animals as creatures lacking conscious
thought and thus part of the great machine of nature put at
the disposal of the human mind.

It is also argued, however, that there is present in the
Christian tradition a parallel and contrasting view of humanity as the "steward" of nature in that "the earth is the Lord's
and the fullness thereof." Basing themselves on the second
account of creation in Genesis, referred to above, many
Christian moralists, theologians, and philosophers—from
those who rejected the Gnostics' antipathy to nature onwards—have defended the view that people have obligations

with respect to many non-humans and that the flourishing of non-humans is of intrinsic value. Even Aquinas, for example, declared: "Every creature exists for its own proper act and perfection.... Furthermore, each and every creature exists for the perfection of the entire universe. Further still, the entire universe, with all its parts, is ordained towards God as its end, inasmuch as it imitates, as it were, and shows forth the divine goodness to the glory of God."[10] It is useful here to distinguish between two traditions, as John Passmore does. He calls them the Stewardship tradition (involving the belief that people are entrusted with a duty to preserve the earth's beauty and fruitfulness) and the tradition of cooperation with Nature (embodying the view that humankind should endeavor to develop and perfect the natural world in accordance with its potentials). The term "cooperation" is perhaps not the right one to use when describing humanity's will to improve nature, i.e., to "make better" in humanity's judgment. Humankind is not a partner in such an enterprise, as the term cooperation would suggest, but rather a tutor with plans and objectives that (so it is believed) will enable nature to reach its full potential. As Passmore points out,[11] the word "nature" derives from the Latin "nascere" which means "to be born" and so describes the potential rather than the actual. So whereas the aim of the seventeenth-century formal garden was to impose the human "esprit geometrique" upon nature with shrubs being pruned to cones and triangles, in the late eighteenth century the aim of the designer was to improve rather than to impose form. Lancelot Brown's nickname "Capability" arose out of his habit of describing a site as "having capabilities"; his task, he thought, was to convert those capabilities into actualities.

The best examples of these different traditions of stewardship and improvement can be found in religious orders such as the Franciscans, the Benedictines, and the Cistercians. Probably no other saint in the history of Christianity has been identified with a reverence for nature more than Francis of Assisi—whom White proposes as patron saint of ecologists.

Saint Bonaventure, the Franciscan theologian who wrote the official biography of St. Francis, wrote of his subject: "When he considered the origin of all things, he would be filled with overwhelming pity, and he called all creatures, no matter how lowly, by the name of Brother or Sister, because as far as he knew, they had sprung from the same original principal as himself."[12] St. Francis has been called an other-worldly mystic characterized by passive humility. While this is exaggerated, it is undoubtedly true that in our scheme of things Franciscans would be regarded as conservationists with a "hands-off" approach to all of creation. In contrast, the Benedictines are the archetypal improvers. Probably no other group has affected the topography of Europe as much as the Benedictine foundations throughout the centuries. By setting up avenues for the cumulative transmission of technological ideas and a brilliant, systematic approach to agriculture, Benedictines certainly figure prominently in an ecological history of Europe. Likewise, the Cistercians, founded by Bernard of Clairvaux, observed the Benedictine rule and were concerned to enhance natural beauty and fruitfulness. The view that we are but a part of a unitary and all-embracing natural order with which we should try to live in harmony is an abiding tradition in Western thought from Erigena and Duns Scotus through Wordsworth, Shelley, Coleridge, and the Romantics to its most striking expression in some of the poetry of Gerard Manly Hopkins. A philosophical counterpart to Hopkins's poetry is to be found in the work of Teilhard de Chardin who set out to formulate an evolutionary metaphysics in which the growing consciousness of humanity would enable it to participate in the self-creation of nature and help it to attain that Omega Point that is its ultimate goal.[13]

Nevertheless, there is in the Western Christian tradition a recalcitrant metaphysical dualism with its picture of God as some sort of substance separate from the world, just as the soul is some sort of substance separate from the body, heaven separate from earth, and humanity separate from nature.

The notion of a self-contained and immutable God has fostered a conception of human beings as instruments of God's will and the natural world as an instrument of human will. In as far as natural objects had any value, it was assigned to them from without.[14] As Jurgen Moltmann has pointed out: "The more transcendent the conception of God became, the more immanent were the terms in which the world was interpreted. Through the monotheism of the absolute subject, God was increasingly secularized. As a result, the human being—since he was God's image on earth—had to see himself as the subject of cognition and will, and was bound to confront his world as its ruler. For it was only through his rule over the earth that he could correspond to his God, the Lord of the world. God is the Creator, Lord and owner of the world."[15] This, in turn, encouraged the view that human beings were in some way metaphysically unique and their salvation metaphysically guaranteed.

From the environmental point of view, the dualistic world view, with its conception that "man" and "nature" are ontologically different realities and that "nature" is simply an instrument for "man" to use, has had noxious effects which are there for all to see. It is worth noting, in addition, that this instrumental view of nature has also fostered the oppression of women. "The ultimate theological rationale for the hierarchical symbolism of masculinity and femininity is the image of God as transcendent Father. Creation becomes the wife or bride of the "sky Father." Most images of God in religions are modeled after the ruling class of society. In biblical religion the image of God is that of patriarchal Father above the visible created world, who relates to Israel as his "wife" and "children" in the sense of creatures totally dependent on his will, owing him unquestioning obedience. This image allows the king and patriarchal class to relate to women, children, and servants through the same model of domination and dependency."[16] And, insofar as women were considered nearer to nature than men they, too, were seen as there to be tamed and exploited. The rape of nature and the rape of women, both metaphorical and literal, has, as part of its enabling background, a certain conception of the relationship between God and the world.

It is, of course, true that other civilizations, inspired by other religions, have made their own contribution to deforestation, erosion, and the general destruction of nature. Historically speaking, however, it is out of the matrix of Latin, and more specifically, Protestant Christianity that emerged the economic juggernaut which regards the earth's natural resources as just there for the taking. Catholicism may have been more lenient towards survivals of pagan animism and even incorporated into its doctrines and practice certain pre-Christian elements, but the zeal of the Reformation, particularly in its Calvinist form, was not so flexible. It propounded a stark man-nature dualism which was a necessary precondition for the Industrial Revolution. This is, of course, the famous thesis of Weber linking the Protestant ethic to the spirit of capitalism. The peculiar type of entrepreneurial spirit fostered by the Calvinist conception of predestination by an utterly transcendent God produced a concomitant psychological urge to consider the accumulation of wealth (but not its spending) as a sign of God's grace. The background to this thesis is the process which Weber, borrowing a phrase from the poet Schiller, called the *"Entzauberung* [disenchantment] of nature."* Whereas nature had from earliest times been full of spirits, it was the achievement of the modern age to drive out the spirits and see nature as a soulless collection of objects ready to be manipulated and exploited by humankind.[17] This view was common ground among most progressive intellectuals around the turn of the century: Herbert Spencer advocated a sub-Darwinian survival of the fittest and Freud set out as his ideal "taking up the attack on nature, thus forcing it to obey human will, under the guidance of science."[18] It is ironical that at the beginning of this century Christians were very keen for their religion to be seen as the origin of science and technology, and now Christianity is being blamed for all the ill-effects of the rapid economic development produced by its offspring. Both Christianity's position of glory and of shame regarding Western technology are undoubtedly exaggerated: however, it is not an accident that technology has flourished in a West where nature has ceased to be sacred.

Although Weber's thesis refers to capitalism, the Green Movement would apply the same strictures to Marxism at least in its classical form since they share the same destructive presuppositions of the *Zeitgeist*. As Simone Weil said: "Marxism is the highest spiritual expression of bourgeois society" which could only express its opposition to that society "in a form determined by the existing order, in a bourgeois form of thought."[19] The early Marx produced fleeting references to the dignity of nature, and the later Engels can sound very green. In his famous essay on *The Part Played by Labour in the Transition from Ape to Man* Engels writes that we should not "flatter ourselves over-much on account of our human victories over nature" since "for each such victory nature takes its revenge on us" and "thus at every step we are reminded that we by no means rule over nature like a conqueror over a foreign people, like someone standing outside nature—but that we, with flesh, blood and brain, belong to nature, and exist in its midst." But even here he is confident that "after the mighty advances made by the natural sciences in the present century, we are more than ever in a position to realise and hence to control even the more remote natural consequences of at least our day-to-day production activities." And his conclusion is that "the more this progresses the more will men not only feel but also know their oneness with nature, and the more impossible will become the senseless and unnatural idea of a contract between man and matter, man and nature, soul and body, such as arose after the decline of classical antiquity in Europe and obtained its highest elaboration in Christianity."[20] This oneness with nature is, however, premised on increasing technological control, with nature yielding to man rather than man to nature. For, central to the Marxist materialist conception of history is the

idea that it is the growth of the productive forces that will
bring about the transition from capitalism to communism
and enable society to use its knowledge for the benefit of all
its citizens. Classical Marxism thus retained a faith in the
beneficent long-term effects of industrialism and economic
development that was every bit as powerful as that of its capitalist opponents. One of the main ideological reasons for the
degeneration of the Russian revolution was their overriding
commitment to the development of the productive forces at
the expense of the relations of production. And the ecological damage that has accompanied the drive for economic
growth in socialist countries has been proportionately as
great as that in the West.

How, then, might these considerations be linked to specific political proposals? The modern ecological movement
only dates back about thirty years to the publication of
Rachel Carson's *Silent Spring* in 1962. And the beginnings of
the movement were dominated by environmentally conscious scientists intent on making information available to
politicians and on writing petitions rather than themselves
organizing politically. There was a tendency, too, particularly
marked in Britain, to see the environmental question as "single
issue" politics which could be incorporated into the present
political system and not as involving a systematic reappraisal
of the foundations of Western political theory; to save the
whale, in other words, rather than restructure the whole of
our political, social, and economic life.

Yet the issues raised by the Green movement cannot be
accommodated within existing Western political traditions.
With its emphasis on one earth, wholeness, and community,
green ideas seem at variance with traditional liberalism. This
is not surprising in that the rise of liberalism parallels that of
the Industrial Revolution. That most exemplary of liberal
thinkers John Stuart Mill was strongly opposed to the idea
that humanity should cooperate with a nature whose powers,
he wrote, "are often towards man in the position of enemies
from whom he must wrest, by force and ingenuity, what little

he can for his own use."[21] The antipathy may seem most evident with the currently dominant market liberalism since it is difficult to see how any society based on the principles of private enterprise could possibly cope with the colossal contemporary threats to our environment. The only resources a market liberal approach has at its disposal are either the extension of property rights, on the grounds that the private owner has an incentive to protect his or her property, or the Chicago School method of incorporating social cost into price on the "polluter pays" principle. If the threats posed by deforestation, global warming, ozone depletion, etc. are only half as great as many scientists suggest, then such approaches will prove totally inadequate.

Almost any other branch of Western political thought, from anarchism on the extreme left to Fascism on the extreme right, has *some* affinity with *some* aspects of green thought.[22] This is obviously so with anarchism, whose principles as expounded by, say, Murray Bookchin fit well with the typical green espousal of decentralized, non-hierarchical participatory society committed to a no-growth economy. Kropotkin and William Morris could be seen as worthy forerunners of Green politics, and St. Francis himself is a true spiritual democrat, some of whose followers—at least as portrayed in *The Name of the Rose*—have distinctly anarchist overtones. At the opposite extreme, certain green themes, such as a distrust of "rationality," lead occasionally to a rather mystical approach, and the call for interventionist measures to limit economic growth and population increase could lead to a centralized and authoritarian politics. Marxists typically see the Green movement as an ally in a broad coalition of groups opposed to capitalist society. But greens would argue that the more fundamental problem is not the exploitation of one class by another but the threat of ecological catastrophe posed by the very nature of industrial societies.

Although it is undoubtedly the socialist tradition that has most in common with contemporary Green politics, the fundamental ecocentrism of green thought does mark it off from

all other political currents. At the same time, it is precisely
that difference and newness that make Green politics difficult to specify in easily recognizable terms. This, of course,
places enormous obstacles to their own political progress.
Since virtually all political discourse is couched in terms of
enlightened self-interest, the turn from anthropocentrism to
ecocentrism demands a revolution in human consciousness
considerably more profound than that demanded by fundamental socialism. But whereas socialists could always claim
that time was on their side, Green political thought cannot:
given the imminence of ecological crisis presupposed, it cannot afford the compromise and accommodation that has
characterized certain sections of the socialist movement.

At the same time, many in the Green movement call for
something that normally takes several generations to come
about: a radical change in consciousness. Some green
thinkers, such as Murray Bookchin, reject anything that
appears to refer to the supernatural and prefer to express
their views solely in the traditional terms of science and
rationality. Most, however, would follow Fritz Schumacher,
the author of one of the classic texts of the green outlook
Small is Beautiful, who called for a "metaphysical reconstruction" and became a Catholic shortly before his death.[23] It is
obvious how much of the language of the Green movement
("pollution" being only the most evident example) has strong
religious connotations. The most prominent of the German
green theorists, Rudolf Bahro, writes that "the differentiation between the creative forces and the forces of inertia
does not take place economically or sociologically but rather
psychologically and in the last instance religiously." This is
because "if we take a look in history at the foundation from
which new cultures were based or existing ones essentially
changed, we always come up against the fact that in such
times people returned to those strata of consciousness which
are traditionally described as religious."[24] Bahro talks of the
need for a new Benedictine community to exemplify the new
approach.

The proclamation of the early Marx, itself simply reflecting the general view of the Enlightenment, the doctrine that "the criticism of religion ends with the doctrine that for man the supreme being is man" has had disastrous consequences for the natural environment. It may be that Christianity has the resources within itself to undo the damage for which it has, in part, been responsible. And there are signs that theologians are seriously addressing themselves to a thorough reevaluation of what it means to think of nature as God's creation.[25] It is in the need for a revolution in consciousness that the connection between religion and politics is at its clearest. The central point in Green politics is that the political, social, and economic problems currently confronting us are a result of our faulty intellectual and spiritual relation with the world and the noxious practices to which this gives rise. These practices go back further than just to the Enlightenment, as the Frankfurt School with its powerful critique of instrumental reason would have us believe. It is our religion itself which is partly responsible. Only some more adequate form of religion is powerful enough to question the myths of science and technical progress that have so gripped the Western imagination and to represent our appropriate relationship to nature. The Jewish and Christian traditions have privileged the personalist rather than the naturalist metaphors of God. Although this personalism is essentially relational (as, e.g., in the Trinity) rather than individualistic, these relations must now be extended to include nature itself.

Notes

1. I am grateful, in this chapter, for the insights gained from the dissertation of Gabrielle Kent, "Environmental Ethics and the Judaeo-Christian Tradition," King's College, London, 1990.

2. S. Weil, *Intimations of Christianity Among the Ancient Greeks* (London: Routledge, 1937), 209.

3. Cf. R. Ayers, "Christian Realism and Environmental Ethics," in *Religion and Environmental Crisis*, ed. E. Hargrove (Athens, Ga.: University of Georgia Press, 1986), 168.

4. For a good overview, see A. Dobson, *Green Political Thought* (London: Unwin Hyman, 1990), chap. 4.

5. L. White, "The Historical Roots of Our Ecological Crisis," *Science* 155 (March 1967): 1203.

6. Ibid., 1207.

7. Cf. S. Bratton, "Christian Ecotheology and the Old Testament," in *Religion and Environmental Crisis*, 64.

8. L. White, "Continuing the Conversation," in *Western Man and Environmental Ethics*, ed. I. Barbour (Reading, Mass.: Addison Wesley, 1973), 60.

9. R. Descartes, *Discourse on Method*, chap. 6.

10. Aquinas, *Summa theologiae* I, q. 65, a. 2.

11. Cf. J. Passmore, *Man's Responsibility for Nature* (London: Duckworth, 1974), 32.

12. *St. Francis of Assisi: The Legends and the Lands,* ed. O. Karrer (London: Macmillan, 1977), 161.

13. For an impressive ecological theology based on Teilhardian principles, see S. McDonagh, *To Care for the Earth: A Call to a New Theology* (London: Chapman, 1986).

14. This thesis is well developed in P. Santmire, *The Travail of Nature* (Philadelphia: Fortress, 1985).

15. J. Moltmann, *God in Creation: An Ecological Doctrine of Creation* (London: SCM Press, 1985), 1.

16. R. Reuther, *New Woman—New Earth: Sexist Ideologies and Human Liberation* (New York: Crossroads, 1975), 74. Also see S. Welch, *Communities of Resistance and Solidarity: A Feminist Theory of Liberation* (Maryknoll: Orbis, 1987).

17. Cf. H. Cox, *The Secular City* (London: SCM Press, 1965), 21.

18. S. Freud, *Civilization and Its Discontents* (London: Hogarth, 1944), 106.

19. Weil, *Oppression and Liberty*, 131. See the same sentiment expressed in R. Niebuhr, *Reflections on the End of an Era* (New York: Scribner's, 1934), 103.

20. K. Marx and F. Engels, *Selected Works* (Moscow: Foreign Languages Publishing House, 1962), vol. 1, p. 365.

21. J. S. Mill, *Nature, the Utility of Religion, and Theism: Three Essays on Religion* (London: Longmans, 1974), 15.

22. Cf. P. Hay, "Ecological Values and Western Political Traditions," *Politics* 8 (October 1988): 22.

23. See further J. Porritt and D. Winner, *The Coming of the Greens* (London: Collins, 1988), chap. 11.

24. R. Bahro, *Building the Green Movement* (Philadelphia: New Society, 1986), 94, 90.

25. See particularly Moltmann, *God in Creation* and, in a more fanciful vein, M. Fox, *The Coming of the Cosmic Christ* (New York: Harper and Row, 1988).

Further Reading

Bahro, Rudolph. *Building the Green Movement.* Philadelphia: New Society Publishers, 1986.

Barbour, Ian. Ed. *Western Man and Environmental Ethics.* Reading, Mass.: Addison Wesley, 1973.

Dobson, Andrew. *Green Political Thought.* London: Unwin Hyman, 1990.

Fox, Matthew. *The Coming of the Cosmic Christ.* New York: Harper and Row, 1988.

Hargrove, E. Ed. *Religion and Environmental Crisis.* Athens, Ga.: University of Georgia Press, 1986.

McDonagh, Sean. *To Care for the Earth: A Call to a New Theology.* London, Chapman: 1986.

Moltmann, Jurgen. *God in Creation: An Ecological Doctrine of Creation.* London: SCM Press, 1985.

Osborn, Lawrence. *Stewards of Creation: Environmentalism in the Light of Biblical Teaching.* Oxford: Latimer House, 1990.

Passmore, John. *Man's Responsibility for Nature.* London: Duckworth, 1979.

Porritt, Jonathan, and David Winner. *The Coming of the Greens.* London: Collins, 1988.

Ruether, Rosemary. *New Woman—New Earth: Sexist Ideologies and Human Liberation.* New York: Crossroads, 1975.

Santmire, Paul. *The Travail of Nature.* Philadelphia: Fortress, 1985.

Spretnak, Charlene. *The Spiritual Dimension of Green Politics.* Santa Fe: Bear and Co., 1986.

Conclusion

As a recent textbook has claimed, "one cannot fully understand how America discharges the function of governing itself without recognising the profound influence of religion."[1] The engaging study of Gary Wills puts it even more strongly: "religion has been at the center of our major political crises, which are always moral crises—the supporting and opposing of wars, of slavery, of corporate power, of civil rights, of sexual codes, of 'the West', of American separatism and claims to empire."[2] And what goes for the United States, goes for most other societies, at least in this respect. But attempts to assess this influence of religion by trying to isolate the religious variable have proved extremely difficult. It is obviously difficult to show that similarities between religious and political views might not be traceable to a third factor—for example, economic and social standing, which, in its turn, could be influenced by religious attitudes as in the classic Weberian thesis.[3] Thus it would not be true to say that, e.g., it is theological conservatism that *produces* traditional responses to social and political questions. It is rather that "traditional religious values are most plausible to people whose limited exposure to the outside world has safeguarded them from the challenge of modern social thought."[4] The most that can be said is that there is a Weberian affinity between certain types of religion and other types of political attitude. For example, there seems to be this sort of correlation between the Jewish religion with its emphasis on learning, on charity, and its lack of emphasis on sin and life after death and the tendency of Jews to be more than averagely

socially active in progressive liberal causes. Similarly, understanding of the Trinity as persons in relation promotes an
analogous understanding of human beings with social and
political implications quite different from the atomist, isolated, non-relational, self-constituting individuals suggested
by Deism and embodied in so much eighteenth-century
political theory and its latter-day followers. The above studies
of the relation of theology to politics in the thought of
Simone Weil, Reinhold Niebuhr, liberation theology, and
Green politics all show evidence of such a connection. This
connection tends, naturally, to be clearer in those whose
world views are more thought through and articulate.

   This claim about the relationship of metaphysics to politics has a parallel in the Marxist tradition. It is at least
arguable that there is close relationship between the politics
practiced by different varieties of Marxism and their acceptance or rejection of the Hegelian dialects. Those who
showed some sympathy for, and understanding of, Hegel's
dialectic tended to emphasize working class consciousness,
class struggle, the self-activity of the working class movement, and to be on the subjective side in general; those who
neglected Hegel tended to put their trust in some sort of natural inevitability about the collapse of capitalism or, while
wishing to intervene actively in history, operated through
some agency not evidently expressive of the consciousness
and desires of the working class. To the first group belong
Marx (most of the time), the later Lenin (in some moods),
Lukacs, Gramsci, and some of the Frankfurt school.
Included in the second group are Engels, Kautsky, Stalin,
and Althusser. In each case the metaphysical background was
formulative of the political attitude and practice.[5] Similarly, it
could be claimed that the ideas of creatureliness, dependency, and consequent responsible recognition of the parent-
hood of God require, politically, a correlative fundamental
option for the poor, whereas the metaphysics of Deism and
of the Cartesian 'ego' is well matched with ideas of individual
self-sufficiency and the pursuit of private property which

help to produce, reinforce, and marginalize social and economic deprivation.

But it might be argued against what is being claimed here, that although the status of religious beliefs may have been important in the past, this importance is declining—and will continue to do so—as the world becomes increasingly secularized. But the whole issue of secularization is an extremely complicated one. The legacy of Marx and Weber still weighs heavily. The worldwide reappearance of religious movements and religious themes over the last two decades should give us pause for thought. The traditional view of social theorists was that the increasing institutional differentiation in societies was removing the old social bonds of community and thus undercutting the bases of religion. Sociologists such as Rowland Robertson, however, are arguing that separate societies are being increasingly integrated into a capitalist world-system which produces a globally social bond affording a new basis for new religious perspectives.[6] The very process of secularization, by separating religion from dominant interests, enables its role to change. The emergence of new social movements, almost all with some sort of religious overtone, illustrates this. The advent of feminist, black, Green, and liberation theologies indicates that religion is part of much of the thinking about the emergent global society and the necessity for finding a genuinely universalist ethic to accompany it. The breakdown of traditional communities has led to the feeling that we no longer enjoy any coherent system of shared values.[7] The advance of technological civilization has bracketed questions of ultimate meaning. The increasing globalization of society may afford opportunities to fill this vacuum.

The role that religion might play in this process is unclear. The very fact that religion has been removed from its roots in traditional social groupings implies that it can now be given extremely diverse meanings and thus used for highly diverse ends. It can, and does, serve as a conservative symbol of national and cultural identity. Equally, it can, and does, serve

as a contestatory symbol of justice, wholeness, and peace.
Much of American religion is undoubtedly of the former
sort.[8] And a Durkheimian functionalist approach to religion
will confirm this view.[9] A more direct account of this version
of Christian values is to be found in Michael Novak's *The
Spirit of Democratic Capitalism* in which "The Trinity
becomes a vision of the importance of individualism over
against the constraints of community; the Incarnation
becomes a reality principle that warns us against the utopian
hopes of socialism; the value of many biblical narratives is
that they 'envisage human life as a contest'; the doctrine of
Original Sin serves mainly to convince us that no economic
system can ever be free of some evil; the doctrine of the Two
Kingdoms becomes an argument for laissez-faire; and the
principle of love in the Judaeo-Christian tradition mainly
suggests that we should respect the freedom of the individual."[10] Christianity, in other words, serves to endorse the
establishment values of competition, this-worldly individual
enterprise, social adjustment, etc. On this view, religion can
provide an over-arching sacred canopy which serves to integrate diverse beliefs under the rubric of "religion of democracy." Religious diversity proved similarly integrative in the
Roman Empire where, according to Gibbon, "the various
modes of worship which prevailed in the Roman world were
all considered by the people as equally true; by the philosopher as equally false; and by the magistrate as equally useful.
And thus toleration produced not only mutual indulgence,
but even religious concord."[11] Religion as symbolic integration and a form of social control is undoubtedly conservative.

   But as well as being the shield of the reactionary, religion
can be the sword of the revolutionary. The Christian message
as harbinger of a radically new society was classically
expressed by Herman Melville in his *Whitejacket*:

   We Americans are the peculiar, chosen people—the Israel of our
   time; we bear the ark of the liberties of the world.... God has pre-
   destinated, mankind expects, great things from our race; and great
   things we feel in our souls. The rest of the nations must soon be in

our rear. We are the pioneers of the world; the advance-guard, sent on through the wilderness of untried things, to break a new path in the New World that is ours.... The political Messiah... has come in *us*, if we would but give utterance to his promptings. And let us always remember that with ourselves, almost for the first time in the history of earth, national selfishness is unbounded philanthropy; for we cannot do a good to America but we give alms to the world.[12]

Fifty years after Melville, however, the dream had begun to fade as "the evangelical consensus became the Protestant Establishment, the chosen nation now smacked of superiority and condescension, the mission of American democracy turned into strident nationalism, and the philosophy of progress was transformed into blatant materialism."[13] But, as the above studies have shown, the potential of the Christian religion for informing a changing world is far from exhausted.

Notes

1. Wald, *Religion and Politics in the United States.*

2. G. Wills, *Under God: Religion and American Politics* (New York: Simon and Schuster, 1990), 25.

3. See the thorough overview of empirical research in R. Wuthnow, "Religious Commitment and Conservatism: In Search of an Elusive Relationship," in *Religion in Sociological Perspective*, ed. C. Glock (Belmont: Wandsworth, 1973).

4. W. Roof, "Religious Orthodoxy and Minority Prejudice: Causal Relationship on Reflection of Localistic World View?" *American Journal of Sociology* 80 (1974): xi.

5. See further D. McLellan, "Religious Alienation and Marxist Critique," *Marquette Journal of Philosophy and Theology* 1, no. 1 (1987).

6. See, for example, R. Robertson and J. Chirico, "Humanization, Globalization, and Worldwide Religious Resurgence: A Theoretical Exploration," *Sociological Analysis* 46, no. 3 (1985), and R. Robertson, "The Sacred and the World System," in *The Sacred in a Secular Age*, ed. P. Hammond (Berkeley: University of California Press, 1985).

7. Cf. A. MacIntyre, *After Virtue* (Notre Dame, Ind.: University of Notre Dame Press, 1984), and M. Ignatieff, *The Needs of Strangers* (London: 1984).

8. See P. Berger, *The Noise of Solemn Assemblies* (New York: Doubleday, 1961), chap. 2.

9. See the classic study of W. Herberg, *Protestant, Catholic, Jew* (New York: Doubleday, 1955).

10. M. Novak, *The Spirit of Democratic Capitalism* (New York: Simon and Schuster, 1982).

11. Gibbon, *Decline and Fall*, vol. 3, p. 278.

12. H. Melville, *Whitejacket* (London: Cape, 1923), 144.

13. R. Linder and R. Pierard, *The Twilight of the Saints: Biblical Christianity and Civil Religion in America* (Downer's Grove, Ill.: Intervarsity Press, 1978), 73.

General Bibliography

Augustine. *The City of God*. 2 vols. London: Dent, 1945.

Becker, Carl. *The Heavenly City of the Eighteenth Century Philosophers*. New Haven, Conn.: Yale University Press, 1932.

Bellah, Robert. *The Broken Covenant: American Civil Religion in Time of Trial*. New York: Seabury Press, 1975.

Bellah, Robert et al. *Habits of the Heart: Individualism and Commitment in American Life*. Berkeley: University of California Press, 1985.

Berger, Peter. *The Noise of Solemn Assemblies*. Garden City, N.J.: Doubleday, 1961.

Blumenberg, Hans. *The Legitimacy of the Modern Age*. Cambridge, Mass.: MIT Press, 1983.

Bruce, Stephen. *The Rise and Fall of the New Christian Right: Conservative Protestant Politics in America 1978–1988*. Oxford: Clarendon Press, 1988.

Chiles, Dennis. *Christianity and Politics*. London: CTS Publications, 1989.

Davis, Charles. *Theology and Political Society*. Cambridge: Cambridge University Press, 1980.

Diggins, John. *The Lost Soul of American Politics: Virtue, Self-Interest and the Foundations of Liberation*. New York: Basic Books, 1984.

Dumas, Andre. *Political Theology and the Life of the Church*. London: SCM Press, 1978.

Forrester, Duncan. *Beliefs, Values and Policies: Conviction Politics in a Secular Age*. Oxford: Clarendon Press, 1989.

———. *Theology and Politics*. Oxford: Blackwell, 1988.

Forrester, Duncan. Ed. *Theology and Practice*. London: Epworth, 1991.

Hatch, Nathan. *The Democratization of American Christianity.* New Haven, Conn.: Yale University Press, 1989.

Herberg, William. *Protestant, Catholic, Jew.* New York: Doubleday, 1960.

James, William. *The Varieties of Religious Experience.* London: 1904.

Kuitert, H. M. *Everything is Politics but Politics is not Everything: A Theological Perspective on Faith and Politics.* London: SCM Press, 1986.

Lash, Nicholas. *Theology on the Way to Emmaeus.* London: SCM Press, 1986.

Linder, Robert, and Richard Pierard. *Twilight of the Saints: Biblical Christianity and Civil Religion in America.* Downers' Grove, Ill.: Intervarsity Press, 1978.

Munby, Denis. *The Idea of a Secular Society and its Significance for Christians.* London: Oxford University Press, 1963.

Neuhaus, Richard. *The Naked Public Square: Religion and Democracy in America.* Grand Rapids, Mich.: Eerdmans, 1984.

Noll, Mark A. Ed. *Religion and American Politics From the Colonial Period to the 1980s.* New York: Oxford University Press, 1990.

Norman, Edward. *Christianity and the World Order.* London: Oxford University Press, 1979.

Novak, Michael. *The Spirit of Democratic Capitalism.* New York: Simon and Schuster, 1982.

Preston, Ronald. *Church and Society in the Late Twentieth Century: The Economic and Political Task.* London: SCM Press, 1983.

Robbins, T., and Roland Robertson. Ed. *Church-State Relations: Tensions and Transitions.* New Brunswick: Transaction Books, 1987.

Toqueville, Alexis de. *Democracy in America.* New York: Vintage, 1945.

Wald, Kenneth. *Religion and Politics in the United States.* New York: St. Martin's Press, 1987.

Walzer, Michael. *The Revolution of the Saints: A Study in the Origins of Radical Politics*. London: Weidenfeld and Nicholson, 1966.

———. *Exodus and Revolution.* New York: Basic Books, 1985.

Weber, Max. *The Protestant Ethic and the Spirit of Capitalism.* New York: Scribner's, 1958.

Wills, Gary. *Under God: Religion and American Politics.* New York: Simon and Schuster, 1990.

Wink, Walter. *Naming the Powers: The Language of Power in the New Testament.* Philadelphia: Fortress Press, 1984.

Wuthnow, Robert. *The Restructuring of American Religion: Society and Faith Since World War II.* Princeton: Princeton University Press, 1988.

Subject Index

Name Index

Acheson, Dean, 38
Ackerman, Bruce, 10
Adam, 73
Althusser, Louis, 60, 88
Aquinas, Thomas, 3, 75
Arendt, Hannah, 34
Aristotle, 60, 74
Assmann, Hugo, 66
Augustine of Hippo, 3

Bahro, Rudolph, 71, 82
Bakunin, Michael, 9
Beauvoir, Simone de, 21
Bellah, Robert, 7
Berdiayev, Nicholas, 6
Bernard of Clairvaux, 76
Bonaventure, Saint, 76
Bonino, Miguel, 61
Bookchin, Murray, 81f.
Brown, Lancelot, 75
Bultmann, Rudolph, 59
Burke, Edmund, 43

Calvin, Jean, 12
Camara, Helder, 55
Cardonnel, Jean, 56
Carson, Rachel, 80
Carter, Jimmy, 1
Coleridge, Samuel, 76

Dawson, Christopher, 6

Descartes, René, 74
Dewey, John, 7
Durkheim, Emile, 7
Dworkin, Ronald, 29

Eco, Umberto, 81
Engels, Friedrich, 79, 88
Erigena, Scotus, 76

Falwell, Jerry, 5
Feuerbach, Ludwig, 43, 65
Ford, Henry, 40
Francis of Assisi, 75f., 81
Freire, Paolo, 55, 65f.
Freud, Sigmund, 78
Fulbrook, Mary, 5

Galileo, Galilei, 5
Gaulle, Charles de, 23
Gibbon, Edward, 90
Gramsci, Antonio, 61, 88
Guttierez, Gustavo, 55f., 58, 66

Hegel, Georg, 62, 88
Hitler, Adolph, 24
Hobbes, Thomas, 3
Hume, Basil, 2

Jackson, Jesse, 5
James, William, 7, 14
Jesus Christ, 9, 12, 57, 63, 73

101